Weaving the Cosmos

Science, Religion and Ecology

Chris Clarke

BOOKS

Winchester, UK
Washington, USA

First published by O-Books, 2010
O Books is an imprint of John Hunt Publishing Ltd., The Bothy, Deershot Lodge, Park Lane, Ropley,
Hants, SO24 0BE, UK
office1@o-books.net
www.o-books.com

For distributor details and how to order please visit the 'Ordering' section on our website.

Text copyright: Chris Clarke 2009

ISBN: 978 1 84694 320 1

A CIP catalogue record for this book is available from the British Library.

Design: Stuart Davies

Printed in the UK by CPI Antony Rowe

We operate a distinctive and ethical publishing philosophy in all
areas of its business, from its global network of authors to
production and worldwide distribution.

Weaving the Cosmos

Science, Religion and Ecology

CONTENTS

Acknowledgments

A great many friends and colleagues have contributed their ideas to this book, but I am particularly indebted to my wife Isabel Clarke for her input on psychology and for her tireless support and help in honing the manuscript.

I am most grateful to Jules Cashford for permission to reproduce her translation of the Homeric Hymn to Artemis.

The front cover — depicting the weaving of the cosmos, including the earth, through the warp and weft of the rational and the spiritual — includes pictures of the galaxy M101, the earth and the Hubble "ultra-deep field" of galaxies, by courtesy of NASA and the Space Telescope Science Institute.

Note to the reader
The word derivations at the start of each chapter come from either the *Oxford English Dictionary*, Lewis and Short's *Latin Dictionary* or Liddell and Scott's *Greek-English Lexicon*

Weaving

There is a woman she weaves the night sky.
See how she weaves, see her fingers fly.
She is the needle and we are the thread.
She is the weaver, and we are the web.
She changes everything she touches,
and everything she touches changes.
She changes everything she touches,
and everything she touches changes.[1]

1

Evocation

*Evoke: To call (a feeling, faculty, manifestation, etc.) into being
or activity. Also, To call up (a memory) from the past....*

I have arrived at the wood.

*When I was first here it was different. I had been driven out of the house
one evening by a thirst (but for what, I did not know) and, wandering
through parks and suburbs finding nothing, I had come here. A tree had
drawn me to itself. Sitting by it for one hour, two hours, I had asked the
questions. I had received answers.*

*Now, some twenty years later, the path I walk along through the
wood is familiar. I am expecting to conduct some tiny ritual, perhaps to
make an offering. But no tree calls. My too noisy footfall startles a deer
that flees through the scrub, its white rump flashing.*

*Memories of previous encounters come to me as I walk: the antlered
deer in another wood where we suddenly met, eye to eye, for an unmea-
surable moment; the answers I received to other questions, at other
trees and rocks, answers arriving suddenly as fully formed thoughts, as
if impressed on my mind by an unfelt stamp, whose meaning only
gradually emerged with time ...*

- "my name is Rainbow"
- "the descent of Spirit into the arms of Matter"

*Now no tree calls, and none is needed. I have already heard, in all these
past events, what is needed.*

Now is the time to write it down.

This book tells what I have learnt over that period of wood-walking, both by personal study and through flashes of intuition – some might say "guidance"– such as I have just described. It is about how the world is, in all its dimensions; it is about how we humans and the planet can flourish together in the future.

A central theme will be the interlinked roles of science and religion. Over the last 100 years science, and particularly quantum theory, has continually developed and has posed more and more radical challenges to old nineteenth century ways of scientific thinking (still perpetuated in much of science teaching today). Over the last 20 years new conceptions of logic and new concepts of reality emerging from quantum theory have opened a window to a way of thinking that is close to the traditional teachings of religion. In the chapters that follow I will describe this convergence of quantum theory and religion, and show how it gives us the mental and spiritual tools for building humanity's future. But I will begin with a reminder of our current human situation, describing the shadows cast over our future which demand this new thinking for their solution.

* * * * *** * * *

In the same way as I have walked through many woods for many years collecting thoughts, so humanity on a grander scale has walked the globe for two hundred thousand years, collecting stories, ideas, skills, theories, rituals, faiths, moral codes, languages ... They accumulate, layer after layer, composting down, building the rich seams of our collective unconscious and our cultural inheritance.

Then, in the last few centuries, these bits of culture come faster and faster, heaping up in high pinnacles of human imagination: science, computer networks, pop music, the iPod, satellites, the internet, globalisation, jumbo jets, super-jumbo jets, the 0.75 trillion dollar pharmaceutical market, the 0.3 trillion dollar illegal drug market ... So many fantastic anarchic constructions.

And all so unstable. The system rocked when Thailand's currency was devalued in 1987, starting the financial dominoes falling across the world in what came to be known as "Black Monday"; and now we are in the midst of the most profound economic turmoil yet, triggered in 2007 when the USA mortgage market revealed its shaky foundations. All these structures stand like castles made of playing cards, wobbling in the tiny jolts of an occasional economic deficit, waiting for the even greater blows to come: the well known blow of climate change, of the end of the oil supply; and the consequent blows of water supplies running out one after the other, of vast migrations of refugees, of rising conflict over dwindling resources ... the blows that may collapse our card castles to the table once and for all.

Here we are then, at a time of the greatest uncertainty humanity has ever faced. Such times of greatest crisis have, of course, come before. But the crises come ever more rapidly; they now are global in scope; the stakes become increasingly higher. Will humanity get through every challenge that we set ourselves up for, scraping through each crisis like the hero in an ongoing James Bond movie? (Except that in this movie humanity is both the villain and the hero.) Or are we speeding towards the final catastrophe, when our species will become extinct, just as we have made so many other species extinct?

I will be arguing that another way of living on this planet is not only possible, but is emerging around us now. It is at first hard for us to understand, because it involves us in acting in a completely different way. For the last 20 years we have been aware of these problems facing us. Many extremely able world leaders have been working hard at overcoming them. But it feels as though we are running up a downward escalator that is getting faster and faster. What I will be suggesting is not that we strain even harder in the direction we are used to, but that we move in a quite different direction.

Two lines of experience convince me of this. The first has been my growing understanding of spirituality and religion, summed up in what the trees and the rocks were "speaking" to me on my walks. The other line of experience comes from my scientific career; investigating new theories in astrophysics, which I was pursuing alongside my walks and my listening. These pointed to a new approach. It is this that I want to write about here: a vision, quietly emerging, that is totally different from what has passed. So different that it is hard to see it, particularly when the media are screaming for more and more of the same. What is emerging is not a vision of a new twist to the economy, though that will be involved; nor a different sort of religion, though it has a lot to do with religion; nor a new scientific theory (the theories that emerged from 1970 to 1998 are enough). It is a vaster vision altogether. A vision of a new sort of humanity inhabiting a restored earth. A vision of a new planetary era. For, once we have fully recognised the power, for good or ill, of the cultural and intellectual structures that we have brought into being, nothing smaller than such a vision will serve us.

Geologists talk about "planetary eras" in the past. In the ancient history of the earth, after the first primitive bacteria life has been through six eras. Each had its own character: eras of algae; of fungi; of strange frond-like animals called ediacara; of invertebrate animals and the great forests than produced coal and oil; of reptiles; and most recently of mammals (like us). Through all these eras, evolution has progressed at its own pace. Species have died out and new species have emerged over time scales of millions of years, driven by the slow processes of natural selection. Now that has suddenly changed. We have realised that the whole climate of the earth, and with it the survival of a large fraction of the species on earth, is in the hands of us humans. Instead of change being controlled by Darwinian evolution, it is now controlled by seven billion human beings. It is our choice what the next planetary era will be like.

We only really woke up to this fact in the last ten years. We had been constructing our mighty cultural and intellectual systems like children, not bothering to think of the consequences. We were playing with all the things we found we could do with the planet. Imagine a bunch of delinquent children playing in a toy store, grabbing the goods they want, spinning them around, throwing them away and grabbing the next one. Wheee! Then the owner of the store appears. Oops – what is he going to say? He looks a bit fierce as he strides towards them, but then he hands over the keys.

"It 's over to you now to run this shop."

What? They were expecting the boss to take control. But it's a whole change of ownership – to the kids.

"Hold it, where's the instruction manual?"

"It's subtle: if I gave it you, you wouldn't understand it. But you'll probably get the hang of it anyway", and he walks off.

This is our condition. It feels as if we are on our own, running the planet without a manual. And about to start a new planetary era as a result.

$$* \quad * \quad * \quad * \quad *** \quad * \quad * \quad * \quad *$$

This book continues the mini-story of the children in toy store that I have just told. How might we "get the hang of " living on the earth while having so much power to destroy it?

What we need is a new story, a story to live by: passionate, credible and transformative of ourselves and the world: a story about what humans are, about how the world is, and about how we live in the world. We had such a story in the past, through religion, myths and legends. But now we have lapsed into a dysfunctional story based on a mechanical universe and human greed. In this sense, we need a new "myth". The scholar of mythology Huston Smith wrote that it takes 4000 years for a new myth to evolve naturally; which is bad news, since many scientists estimate that we have 10-20 years before human activities will lead to irreversible changes to our planet, imperilling the whole of civilisation. We cannot just wait for the new story that is needed. Instead we need to dip deep into our existing myths for the wisdom that lies there, and draw strongly on what science is telling us now, in order to make a story with authenticity – one that can be respected as a story for our age.

I shall be looking in detail at the key ideas that will be needed for this new story; but let me give you a preview of the problem it has to address, and of the solution.

The good news, which is part of the solution, is that we humans are fantastically ingenious and creative. We have tackled huge problems in the past and shown that we can usually fix things provided everyone involved behaves responsibly.

The bad news is that everyone doesn't behave responsibly; this is the problem. And this is ultimately not a matter of wickedness, or bad upbringing, or mental derangement (though there is plenty of that around): it is a consequence of the very creativity that makes us human beings what we are. The problem lies in the basic nature of being human. Yet there is a shift that we can make, a "getting the hang of it", like suddenly learning to ride a bicycle, that can turn our human nature from the problem into the solution.

There is one vital key to getting the hang of living: it lies in connecting with the natural world. The direction in which we have been struggling to travel recently had been one where most people feel disconnected from the natural world, and discon-nected from each other; and this at a time when we need to heal the natural world and when we need solidarity with each other. The new direction needs to be one where we rediscover these connections that we have lost. And the most powerful one is the connection with the world, using the deeper senses of our bodies, and the deeper instincts of our minds.

I will illustrate this with a longer story – in fact, a myth: one of those fundamental stories that crops up in many forms and teaches a basic truth about the way things are – the Greek myth of Eros and Psyche[2]. Many writers have told this story in many different ways (I will be using the ideas of one of these writers, Freya Matthews, later in this book). Here is yet another, less usual perspective.

* * * * **** * * * *

My name is Psyche. I was the youngest daughter of the king and queen of a city whose name and place is now forgotten. My two older sisters were, you might say, good looking. I remember how my father easily obtained husbands for them, princes from the other nearby city-state. The princes arrived, bowed proudly before my sisters, delivered their elegant speeches and in due course made "good matches". All that proceeded satisfactorily.

But it was different with me. No, I wasn't ugly: if there had been a wicked fairy around at my conception, it wasn't this that she cursed me with. It was with beauty, the greatest beauty in the world. I remember the suitors who came to visit me; how they crossed the threshold, trembled, then knelt and worshipped: worshipped me, a girl, barely a woman. All thoughts of statecraft and strategy fled from them, as they joined the growing crowd of ecstatic devotees in my father's kingdom. I could do nothing about it. I felt helpless and increasingly depressed at what seemed a hopeless situation. My father and mother, who truly loved me, were at their wits end, finding an unstoppable cult of worshippers growing up around us.

And then came the oracle. My parents had gone to consult the god Apollo, who spoke through a prophetess at a sanctuary several days journey from our city. When they returned, their drawn faces and their tears told me everything I needed to know. A great numbness closed around me during the following days of preparation for what was to be both my wedding and my funeral. I can remember little of the final day but the endless sound of wailing and weeping at dawn as I climbed the slope to the top of the cliffs bordering the sea. Then all the winds in the

7

world swept down in a tornado that lifted me and whirled me into oblivion.

When I came to, I found to my surprise that I was not dead, but lying unharmed on a sandbank in a bay encircled by hills. A single small house stood on the shore, built of a translucent marble whose glowing inner colours changed with the changing sun. I walked the path towards it, lined with pineapples, pomegranates and a hundred other fruits I had never seen before; past carved basins flowing with spring water, through softly furnished rooms opening to trees filled with birdsong. But never a sign of any other human.

Here I lived in a kind of constant dream, with all I could want showered on me throughout the day. And in the night, in a room so completely dark that I could not tell if my eyes were opened or closed, He came. What at first was a terror, became a sweetness that my body longed for more with every passing day.

Yet thoughts from the past kept invading my dreamy existence, memories of what I had heard of the oracle of Apollo, imaginings of what my sisters might be saying: that I was married to a hideous serpent, that I was doomed to live this dream for ever, that I had given up my freedom for a dream ... and more and more there came into my mind the idea that I should kindle a light in the darkened room, look at Him, and discover the reality of my fate.

You may know the outcome, from the titillating pictures of your Victorian painters: two naked lovers, each radiantly beautiful, the man Eros asleep with a shimmer of wings about his shoulders, the woman (that was me) holding over him a lighted oil lamp, and with trembling hand spilling one drop of searing hot oil on his shoulder. He awoke from his sleep, I awoke from my dream-like state. He fled in pain, and all the harsh reality of the world rushed upon me. I realised that the bliss I had known was gone forever; that I was left with nothing.

In anguish I wandered out of the bay onto the high banks of a swirling river, wanting only to end my life. But in the moment when I threw myself towards the river, I saw its sparkling surface and the greenness of the bordering plants, I heard the music of its waves, and *felt my arms open to embrace the river. Instead of my death, I met an answering surge of water that lifted me onto the bank, where I lay, my misery now mixed with a spark of gratitude.*

A flock of goats was ambling past me beyond the bank. Among them was a man wearing goat skins who, despite the age marked in his wrinkled face, was stepping so lightly and swiftly that I had at first mistaken him for one of the goats. He looked at me, his eyes full of knowing and understanding. "There is no need of death," he said. "Only hold to whom you love." And he continued his way, leaving behind in me a germ of hope from the wisdom of the goats.

It was to be a long time before this hope came to fruition. For the next two days I wandered up the river valley with little idea what to do, trying only to survive, carried forward by love for the one I had lost. A perplexed inner dialogue was going round and round in my mind.

"Who are you, Love" I asked, "that you bring me such suffering?"

"Who are you, wretch" Love replied, "that you think bliss lasts forever? Who are you, that you defame the name of love by giving up in adversity?"

"But how can I, a young woman, understand what to do?"

"Yet understand it you must, before the night is passed."

I had stopped to rest in a ruined barn, where some sacks of wheat and peas had been thrown down and burst onto the soil, the wheat and the peas lying uselessly mixed. To understand my human condition was as difficult, it seemed to me, as to separate out these seeds by hand before the night fell. Then I noticed the ants, running around the barn. They were of two species, from different nests, and one species was carrying off the peas and the other the wheat, in two continuous untiring processions. Nature could accomplish what seemed to me impossible. Night fell, and for the first time brought a little more peace of mind.

But the next day brought rain, swept through the barn by a chilling wind, soaking my thin summer clothes in minutes and, on top of my growing hunger, reducing me again to giving up in despair. Again I turned to the river bank to drown myself. This time I was saved by a single reed, bobbing rhythmically in the wind, saved by the perfection of the seeds sprouting from its tip, by the intricate patterns of green lines threading its stem that caught my eye. How could I give up, in a world that contained such joyful beauty?

This was the turning point for me. Much more was to happen, and I was to sink even lower, to Hades, before I finally gained full understanding through the aid of a majestic eagle that carried me on his back. But perhaps I have said enough to give you the flavour of my journey. It has been sung by many bards, and in your world you can read the rest of the story in your books and even on your computers

.

*   *   *   *   *   ***   *   *   *

Psyche's problem is, at one level, the problem faced by every woman and man growing up. She takes the step of discovering her body, her sexuality, but this discovery remains "in the dark", unconnected with her rational side. It is also a private enjoyment, cut off from the problems of the world at large. Indeed, her sexuality, rather than inspiring her to move forwards, holds her back in a blissful dependence like an infant at the breast. When her condition becomes impossible, she is led forward, not by her own ingenuity (which totally fails her), but by encounters with the larger world of nature. This physical world speaks to her body rather than her rational intellect, – but although it is at first alien to this princess, she starts to see Nature as something that relates to her and which she can relate to. She learns to see it not as a chaotic "otherness" but as a world with its own ways of being, which she can respond to and benefit from. She learns from this how her own rationality can work in harmony with her physicality as part of the greater web of life.

The word "psyche" in Greek means "soul", from which we derive words like "psychology". It is the seat of thought and reflection. "Eros" represents the principle of feeling and yearning, from which we derive "erotic". The story underlines the dangers of the separation of thinking and the feeling, and the way in which they can be brought together in wisdom.

The meaning of the story is that connecting with the world and connecting the parts of our self are inseparable. You cannot have one without the other. The transformation I am talking about consists simply of learning to enter relationship. This necessarily involves becoming a whole person, connecting within ourselves, and connecting with the world. Again, you cannot have one without the other.

In retelling the story I have cut out many strands of the plot and only covered a small part of the history. Also I have made one big change, from which smaller changes follow: I have cut out the gods! In the original, Eros is a god, the goatherd is the god Pan, and Love is the goddess Aphrodite who appears to Psyche and sets her a series of tasks. Separating the seeds is the first of several. I pushed out the gods because the idea of the Greek and Roman gods now seems strange to us. Indeed, there are good reasons in our current culture for trying to see beyond these super-people who were thought to be responsible for running bits and pieces of the world. This notion was a passing phase in humanity's evolution, even though it still lives on in aspects of modern religions.

But the gods bring to the story two vital elements that we need to recover in the pages to come[3]. First, the gods symbolise in a vivid way the various principles and themes that govern human existence, which we may be in danger of forgetting. But second, and much more importantly, missing out the gods leads to the danger of eliminating "the sacred". This difference between the sacred and the gods is vital. It will be one of our major concerns in the chapters ahead. A god does not merely explain some feature of the universe or symbolise some principle of existence; a god, or God, also points beyond itself, beyond ourselves, to a completely different way of knowing the world. The writers of tales of the gods were trying to convey this. One phrase for the quality that opens this way of knowing to us is "the sacred"; another, which I will use in this book because it has fewer difficult associations, is *the numinous*. It means a quality of power, specialness, or ultra-reality. It is an experience, a feeling (but more than a feeling) that can come across us, sometimes when we are least expecting it.

The numinous can be deceptive and lead us wildly astray. But it can also be a way of knowing truths that are hard or impossible to put into words. This is the treasure concealed within religions which, alongside the theme of connecting with nature, enables us to live in the new era that we are creating. So in this book I want to "have my cake and eat it": to go beyond the concepts of gods that were dominant in classical Greek and Roman times by taking a scientific approach to the world; but also to retain the way of knowing associated with the numinous and contained in religions. Not only that; I want to show that this combination of science and the numinous is essential if we are to accomplish the connection with the natural world that I am calling for. Just as Psyche had to bring together rational thinking and erotic feeling, so humans now have to bring together science and religion.

But I will have a lot of explaining to do: explaining what I mean by science, what I mean by the numinous, how they fit together and how this helps us organise our world. In this chapter of evocations, suggestions of the ideas that are to come, I will give a few tasters of what is to come, starting with religion.

*　*　*　*　***　*　*　*

Religion is important, complex and, above all, personal: it affects how people feel and act. So it is appropriate for me to explain religion by describing how it has affected me personally, and how I have come to understand its different aspects. This will also help to explain my approach to religion in this book.

I was brought up as an atheist. My mother – the dominant

parent in my childhood – had lost her father at an early age and had been brought up by her mother, an admirer and supporter of the "suffragettes" who had campaigned for the rights of women to vote for members of parliament. Although an atheist, my mother had many religious aspects to her thinking. She was highly moralistic, and (as I discovered much later) she had experienced moments of intense connection with nature that had moved her and puzzled her. She was intrigued by religion, to the point of deciding that it probably was in some way "a good thing", and started attending church later in her life.

So the values of independence, radicalism, morality and a sort of middle class socialism were passed down to me. I started off with the inheritance of a great curiosity about life, about what makes everything tick, and a great desire to find out things for myself, not taking anyone else's answers for granted. First and foremost this led me to science, but I was also interested in religion and had become a sort of weak Buddhist at school. At university, where I studied mathematics and physics, I was ready prey to two contrasting influences: the college "Christian Union", a fervent evangelical group, and "the Guild of the Holy Name", an intellectual high church group at the opposite end of the spectrum of Christian practices. With the Christian Union I attended meetings full of extempore prayer all about being "born again", and with the Guild I chanted plainsong and celebrated the Catholic festivals. Both had a lot to do with the feeling of numinosity.

It was the Christian Union who first gained the upper hand in this mixture, when I followed their suggestions and was, in retrospect unsurprisingly, rewarded with the sort of conversion experience which they expected. I first miserably acknowledged my sinful state (a concept bequeathed from my mother's morality), and after holding this for many hours one night I rebounded into a joyful acceptance of the removal of my sinfulness by Jesus. I imagined Jesus as physically present, with a vividness that, when accompanied by the emotions of joy, became almost a vision. I was a Believer! Now I too could join in their prayers and thanksgiving. But I in no way gave up my other interests. I continued in the sciences, in the Guild of the Holy Name and in my intellectual curiosity. Indeed most of my subsequent life has been shaped by these latter strands. I progressively understood more and more about what religion was and how it fitted in with other human activities. Most of my exploration has been within the Christian religion. I will be writing mainly about this, because it is what I know most about, though I will often draw from other religions

I was, as just noted, a Believer; and some readers may be wondering whether I still am. So now is a good time to say a bit about "belief". The sort of belief that I was led into at university was an emotional affair that had a lot to do with the "feeling and yearning" that Psyche had when she was with Eros. She needed to connect this feeling with her thinking. In the same way I, after my conversion, set out on the path of connecting belief with science.

"Belief" is actually quite an elusive idea (I deal with it at length in Chapter 3). The Greek word used in the original New Testament, which can be translated either as "belief" or "faith" depending on the context, occurs about 430 times, if you count its various grammatical variations. In most of these cases it is used in a sense reminiscent of my conversion experience. Take, for instance, the typical story, found in three of the four Gospels, of the official whose household servant (or in one version, his son) was ill. He had heard of the miraculous healer, Jesus, and so he came to beg Jesus to come and heal the boy. Jesus does not go to the boy, but simply declares to the official that he will live. The official returns home, finds the boy alive and well, and enquires when he had recovered. "Then the [official] realized that this was the exact time at which Jesus had said to him, 'Your son will live.' So he and all his household *believed*."

The story describes a "Wow experience". It was a situation of high emotion; the official is portrayed as being very fond of the boy; the healing, at long range, is more miraculous than usual; at this highly charged moment not only the official but everyone involved has their attitudes suddenly turned around and they relate to Jesus in a new way. It is not "belief" as in believing that vitamin C will stop you getting a cold, but "belief" in the sense of conversion. The key thing about this "belief" is not deciding that certain facts are true (though this may also happen), but undergoing a psychological turning. And because Christianity is a religion in which devotion to Jesus is commonly an important part, the psychological change is focused around the person's relationship to Jesus. Emotion has a part in this, but it is the change in relationship that defines the moment of belief.

To answer the question I alluded to just now, I am still a Believer, in the sense that the figure of Jesus remains someone that I can relate with, but my belief has steadily evolved and become richer over the years. It underwent a sudden enlargement some 20 years ago when I attended a personal development workshop based on the ideas of Wilhelm Reich. He held, among other things, that traumatic events in our past that blocked our ability to live psychologically healthy lives, leave their marks in the structures of our bodies. So stimulating the body could release these blocks and generate new and healing patterns of action. Reich called these blocks in the body "armouring". At the workshop which I attended we carried out a simple massage exercise in pairs, which for me released a whole spectrum of emotional responses that had been blocked since early childhood. Having been living in my brain for the previous 30 years, I now greeted my body with delight and started to make friends with myself.

I was now on the path that Psyche had been on, of connecting the separated parts of my person, and I started looking for all the signposts that I could find to direct me how this was to be done.

An early find was the teaching of the Christian priest Matthew Fox. He emphasised the role of the material world in spirituality: the role of the body in living and in worship, and the role of the whole natural world in revealing God. Thus a connection with nature entered my spirituality, and has stayed with me ever since. It became even clearer to me that religion and belief was not merely an intellectual matter, but involved relationship at its core; and relationship involved the body. Chapter 3 below will be devoted to exploring how all this alters the way in which we think about religion.

* * * * *** * * * *

My love of science grew and developed through all of this, at first in parallel with religion, and then increasingly as linked with religion. Science is driven by curiosity: I wanted to *know* ... how the universe fitted together, how the forces of nature worked, how the human mind worked. And I was particularly attracted to the challenging, puzzle-solving activity of mathematical physics as one way of knowing about these things. I specialised in the theory of gravitation (known as General Relativity), following in the footsteps of Stephen Hawking who was a few years ahead of me at the University of Cambridge. I eventually became a professor in the mathematics department of the University of Southampton, leading a research group in this area.

A couple of chance conversations then gave an important new twist to my life. The first was with the radical biologist Rupert Sheldrake, whom I had got to know while at Cambridge. He happened to be corresponding with a practitioner of Complementary Medicine in Southampton who was interested in acupuncture, and was trying to understand how it worked in terms of Western science. What happened to the body when one inserted acupuncture needles? Could you detect changes in the places where, according to traditional Chinese theory, the "meridians" that carried vital energy were supposed to run?

To try and answer questions like these, this practitioner was working with a scientist in the physics department of my own university. The department had developed new techniques for detecting the minute magnetic fields generated by human body as it goes about its business of sending electrical pulses through our nervous system. I went along to see how this was done, and found that the most interesting application of this new technology was in detecting the magnetic fields produced by the brain. In principle, this could give one information about what was going on deep in the human brain, without the need for any surgical interference. The problem was, how could one calculate what was going on in the nerves deep in the brain from a knowledge of the magnetic fields that this produced outside the brain?

I realised that this problem was mathematically equivalent to what I was then doing in gravitation theory, working out how what was going on in a star changed the gravitational field around it. The star was a sphere, while the brain was (more or less) a hemisphere; the magnetic field and the gravitational field obeyed similar sorts of equations; so moving from one to the other was a straightforward matter. For the next couple of years I found myself contributing to medical studies of the human brain, focussing particularly on epilepsy.

This led to the second conversation, with the neuro-psychiatrist Peter Fenwick. He was interested in my work; but the real problem, he told me, was consciousness. How could one go from all these electric currents in the brain, which I had been studying, to *being aware* of a world around you? You could work out how signals from the eyes came into the brain, and make guesses at the sort of things that might happen as the brain processed these and, like a super-computer, generated impulses to the muscles as a result; but where did awareness come in? Where was "I" in all this?

As I was to discover, this was, and still is, one of the most hotly contested areas of psychology and philosophy. According to one school of thought, this question is the most difficult and the most important in philosophy today. According to the other school of thought, it isn't a meaningful question at all, but just a silly muddle, because there is really no such thing as an "I", just a lot of nerve cells in a brain, and "awareness" is just another name for a particular process happening among these nerve cells. The whole controversy suddenly connected together my physics and my body-centred spirituality and religion. In one way or another it has preoccupied me ever since. Understanding this question will play a vital part in building a vision for the new planetary era.

These themes of ecology, religion, science and, above all, the mythical theme of the connection of the intuitive and the rational through Pan will be developed into a practical vision of how humanity can now, if we so choose, "grow up" into harmony with the earth.

2

Weaving

In the last chapter I wrote about connecting the separated parts of ourselves – intuition and rationality – and connecting with nature. I argued that these are inseparable: it is all about achieving wholeness. I likened humanity today to teenagers treating our planet like a discardable toy. We have yet to fully grow up and achieve this wholeness. In the pages ahead I will be describing how we started to grow up over the preceding centuries, through developments in science and religion, and how these have now brought us to the point where wholeness is completely within our grasp, as individuals and as a society. Although entering the new era involves a radically new direction, it is a direction that we are ready to take.

Religion and science involve us in understanding the meaning of the whole world and our place in it. There will be many pieces in the jigsaw: philosophy, myths, physics and the study of how we think: that is, logic and psychology. But the notion of the wholeness of rationality and intuition is the simple key to it all. "Growing up" for humanity consists in taking such firm grasp of this wholeness that we become conscious of it in all areas of our existence. These many facets then all fit together into the most remarkable picture that humanity has ever seen. So next I will describe this key in greater depth.

*   *   *   *   *   ***   *   *   *   *

We are considering two opposite poles of thinking, which I am loosely calling **intuition** and **rationality,** woven together by a dynamic flow[4] which, equally loosely, I will call **wisdom**.

Let me say a bit more about each of these in turn.

By "intuition" I mean something very general. At the simplest level, it is the way in which, in minute-to-minute ordinary life, ideas come to us without our having to think about it. In writing this book, every so often there is a pause, a moment of "I'm stuck, what next?" and then the pattern starts to flow again. This fairly low-level intuition can, at even simpler levels, merge into those mechanical tasks like driving a car which we carry on automatically. At higher levels the "stuckness" and the question may be sharper, and the answer may come with more force and clarity. What shall I say to this difficult person I am about to meet? How can I best "recharge my batteries" at this moment? Or it might be that the knowing of what to do comes more continuously and effortlessly, when I am "in the flow" and I find myself smoothly taking the right decisions one after another. Or, at a higher level still, I might become aware of what is needed in a way that is not comprehensible to me, coming surprisingly – as in the instances of receiving important inspirations about my future life in ritual circumstances which I described at the start of the last chapter.

At times these more powerful intuitions might be so unexpected that they seem to come from an external agency, which we might name as "god" or "angel" if our traditions leads us to think in that way. Or they might seem to be the result of a capacity for knowing that is different from ordinary sensation. Examples of this come from people in indigenous cultures, as in this example of the intuition of an elder of Gwich'in Nation, of Yukon:

> "My mother would get up early. She would go outside and stand there a long time. Then she would say, "Vehsih yehno nah ha ooh." That means. "The caribou are just under the mountains over there, and they're coming." Everyone would get excited."[5]

These examples are very diverse, because I am using the word "intuition" in this book as a shorthand for many very different ways of knowing that we humans possess in addition to rational, verbal thinking. I must stress this point, because "intuition" is normally used to mean only what happens when we get a strong mental "hunch" about something. In the context of the study of religion, for instance, the scholars of religion Jorge Ferrer and Jacob Sherman[6] list such ways of knowing as imagination, knowing through feelings in our body including erotic feelings, discerning through empathy with another person or another non-human being, moral awareness in which we respond to a feeling of value and rightness, our aesthetic response to patterns embodying beauty or horror, discovery through meditation or contemplation, and many more. As I will explain in chapter 9, the reason for separating all these diverse ways of knowing from rationality is that, though coming from many different sources, they appear to be all brought together into a single system in our brain: a system concerned with forming and maintaining our networks of relationships with the whole world around us, in both its social and environmental dimensions. Philip Barnard, the cognitive scientist who carried out the research, calls the product of this system "Implicational meaning". He writes:

"Implicational meaning ... is latent meaning rather than artic-ulated meaning. It integrates over sensory, bodily and ideational [to do with imagination] dimensions to create among other things, elaborate schematic models of the self as construed in ideation, in a body state and in an environmental context. It supports generic senses of knowing or 'intuitions'. Implicational meaning can be [emotionally] charged, and equates with a sense of 'knowing with the heart'."[7]

When I talk about "rationality", which is at the opposite pole to intuition, I refer to all those mental activities that are involved, directly or indirectly, with language. In this mode we sit down and debate with ourselves what to do, rather than waiting for the answer to appear. Usually this activity goes on at the same time as intuition: talking to ourselves can clear the ground so that a more intuitive idea can appear. In fact our normal functioning is one in which words, or word-like concepts (rationality), flow seamlessly with non-verbal intuitions. It is only through careful psychological experimentation that it is possible to distinguish two quite separate mental processes at work here. We share intuition with our mammalian relatives, while the rational involves specifically human faculties. At a more specialised level, "rationality" can also mean using words carefully and logically, a topic that we will examine later on.

While rationality and intuition can be fairly well defined, the flow that connects them is less easy to pin down. I have chosen the word "wisdom" to refer to this flow in order to indicate quite a wide range of possibilities. At the psychological level it can refer to the processes, still rather shadowy, that operate in the brain in order to link the rational and the intuitive. We will meet these in chapter 9 under the name of "the central engine of cognition".

More generally, "wisdom" refers to our ability to weigh up the validity of our intuitions and calculations; for both can come up with ideas that are completely batty! Within the world of therapeutic approaches to mental health this corresponds to the "wise mind" of Linehan's Dialectical Behaviour Therapy, which she defines as

"that part of each person that can know and experience truth. It is where the person knows something to be true or valid. It is almost always quiet, It has a certain peace. It is where the person knows something in a centered way."[8]

It is often experienced as much in the body as in our thoughts.

22

Tania Dolley[9] has described how this knowing allows us to draw wisdom from the natural world, as we have seen in the myth of Eros and Psyche. In particular, she cites Carl Rogers' term 'organismic experience' [which] refers to that sense of bodily knowing beyond intellectual understanding. Rogers describes a 'fully-functioning person' as being congruent with this organismic experience or bodily felt sense, and open to 'the sensory and visceral experiencing which is characteristic of the whole animal kingdom'[10].

The word "Wisdom" also links with the personification of Wisdom in the Hebrew scriptures. She appears as the creative force in the universe, as well as being available to human beings in their everyday lives:

> "I [Wisdom] was there when [God] set the heavens in place, when he marked out the horizon on the face of the deep, when he established the clouds above and fixed securely the fountains of the deep, when he gave the sea its boundary so the waters would not overstep his command, and when he marked out the foundations of the earth. Then I was the craftsman at his side. I was filled with delight day after day, rejoicing always in his presence"[11].

I will represent this triad in a diagram:

Rationality ← Wisdom → Intuition

It is a key that is reflected in many different ways in different aspects of our existence. It is reflected in the make-up of our brains, and because of this it is reflected in our myths, where these terms becomes characters like the trio of Eros, Psyche and Pan whom we have already met. Surprisingly and importantly it is reflected in the core structures of matter, in fundamental physics and in the physical aspects of nature that flow from this, as I will explain in Chapter 8. I would speculate that this is not a coincidence: quite probably our brains have evolved with a structure that fits with the way of the universe so that we are able to live more effectively within that "way".

I think of wisdom as moving backwards and forwards between rationality and intuition, like the shuttle on a loom, weaving these two together. As we progress, different forms of this triad will emerge in many different aspects of existence: our mental world, the physical world, the world revealed in the experiences of the mystics ... In all these we can see the same weaving together of opposites. This is the cosmos, weaving itself.

In this chapter I want to describe a second mythological reflection of the basic triad: the character of Artemis (or Diana, as she is called in Roman mythology) and her compatriots Apollo and Gaia.

*   *   *   * *** *   *   *   *

Myths belong to the realm of dreams, where images are linked by association. In this realm each image is as likely to be associated with its opposite as with a similar image. This tendency to link opposites[12] is, as we shall see later, characteristic of the logic of both the human mind and of quantum physics, so myths can be our guide into both the inner world of our mind and the outer world of science. The myths surrounding Artemis are full of imagery of the union of opposites: of light and darkness, high and low, gentleness and violence, earth and heaven, land and sea.

Her mother was Leto and her father the notoriously unfaithful Zeus. His wife Hera in her jealousy cursed Leto, that she could give birth neither on land nor sea nor on an island; and so she gave birth on the floating pseudo-island of Delos – a place of the union of opposites. Hesiod described Leto as "dark-gowned Leto, always mild, kind to men and to the deathless gods, mild from the beginning, gentlest in all Olympos". Her kindness suggests

light, and she is the daughter of Phoebe the goddess of light
(Phoebos means "shining"), but her dark gown suggests
darkness and she is often depicted with a half drawn veil,
suggesting a mixture of revealing and concealment. She is paired
with the depths, in that she was attacked by the serpentine
monster Typhon, who was worshipped at Delphi where he lived
in the depths of the rock, the son of Gaia (Earth) and Tartarus
(the god of the ultimate depths "as far beneath Hades as heaven
is high above earth"[13]).

Leto's son Apollo, brother of Artemis, defeated Typhon and
took over Typhon's shrine at Delphi. But the line of priestesses
who delivered the oracles at the shrine (which appeared in the
myth of Psyche in the last chapter) still sat over a cleft in the rock,
inhaling psychedelic fumes from the depths as they had in the
days of Typhon. Apollo was identified with light and learning.
He was the God of music and poetry and leader of the Muses
(minor deities who were the sources of artistic inspiration).

Artemis unifies the opposites expressed by Typhon and
Apollo, and hinted at in the character of her mother. She is the
choreographer of the gods, and so has the aesthetic power of
Apollo. But she is also the goddess of hunting: her most typical
pose shows her in a strong, balanced posture resting her hand on
a stag, at one with herself and with the wildness of nature. She
is a virgin, in the ancient sense of one who is vowed to independence and self-possession. For me, the definitive statement of the
role of Artemis is the "Hymn to Artemis", probably composed in
the 5th century BCE, which I give here in Jules Cashford's translation[14]:

Artemis I sing
with her golden arrows
and her hunting cry
the sacred maiden
deer-huntress

showering arrows
sister of Apollo
with his golden sword.

In mountains of shadow
and peaks of wind
she delights in the chase,
she arches her bow
of solid gold

she lets fly
arrows
that moan

Crests
of high mountains
tremble,
the forest
in darkness
screams
with the terrible howling
of wild animals

the earth itself shudders,
even the sea
alive with fish

But the heart of the goddess
is strong,
she darts everywhere
in and out, every way
killing
the race of beasts.

Weaving

And when she has had enough
of looking for animals,
this huntress
who takes pleasure in arrows,
when her heart is elated,
then she unstrings
her curved bow

and goes
to the great house
of Phoebus Apollo,
her dear bother,
in the fertile grasslands
of Delphi
and there she arranges
the lovely dances
of the Muses and Graces

There she hangs up
her unstrung bow
and her quiver of arrows,
and gracefully
clothing her body
she takes first place
at the dances
and begins

With heavenly voices
they all sing

they sing of Leto
with her lovely ankles,
how she gave birth
to the best children

of all the gods,
supreme
in what they say
and do.

Farewell
children of Zeus and Leto,
she of the beautiful hair.
Now
and in another song
I will remember you.

Here Artemis is portrayed as one who moves between the two opposite realms of Heaven (The great house of Phoebus Apollo) and Earth (Mountains of shadow), corresponding to her two roles as choreographer of the gods and goddess of hunting. Heaven and earth are given opposite characteristics:

Heaven:

Light. "Phoebus" (shining) is the name of the grandmother of Artemis.

Grace, culture. "gracefully clothing her body", "the lovely dances".

Creating order. "arranges the dances", "takes first place"

Earth:

Darkness. "mountains of shadow" ... "the forest in darkness".

Physicality and spontaneity. "her hunting cry" ... "she delights" ... "the heart ... is strong"

Chaos. "she darts everywhere - in and out, every way", "the terrible howling of wild animals"

Two points stand out from the original Greek text, in relation to what we will be looking at later. First, "forest" is *hylē*

28

(pronounced – very approximately – "hulair"), which when the poem was written meant "woods", but which soon afterwards came to mean "matter". So the poem stands at the moment when "matter", the main concept in the development of science, starts to emerge as distinct concept.

Second, the word for "earth" used later in the poem is *Gaia*, the anciently revered Earth Mother who is also the Python's mother. Today the word "Gaia" has been brought back in the form of "The Gaia Hypothesis" – the term used by the scientist James Lovelock for his discovery that the whole earth behaves like a living organism, in the way that it regulates itself and responds as a whole to any changes. Lovelock has brought "Gaia" into the modern ecological debate, along with the ancient resonances of Gaia, who in this poem is one of the two poles that Artemis weaves together.

The poem stands as a pivot between two ages of history: the archaic age before the poem, when dance, story, action, creation and destruction were a seamless whole; and the cultured age of cities that was by the fifth century BCE detaching itself from the physicality of the earth. The poet's language paints the contrast between earth and heaven, but also allows the character of Artemis herself to be manifest; she for whom there is no contrast or division, who moves seamlessly between the two worlds which, to civilised man, seem poles apart. The rational divides, the intuitive unites, and both are necessary. Lines from the Sufi poet Rumi describe the way this weaving of the worlds of heaven and earth touch us personally:

Once again a moon descends to earth
(don't go back to sleep)
People are going back and forth across the doorsill
where the two worlds touch:
the door is round and open:
don't go back to sleep.[15]

29

*   *   * * *** *   *   *   *

So we now have two myths to work with. The story of Psyche, Eros and Pan which depicts the struggle for unity-in-difference within the human personality; and the figure of Artemis who depicts this same struggle at the cosmic level. These are the inner and the outer mythological reflections of the dynamic between intuition and rationality. So we can augment our rather abstract diagram with these two more vivid embodiments of it:

Outer

Apollo ⟵ Artemis ⟶ Gaia

Inner

Psyche ⟵ Pan ⟶ Eros

These, and other variations that will follow, are all different expressions of a single triad that determines how we perceive the world. We will be looking at this basic psychological triad in the next chapter.

Later we will examine the way the weaving, flowing process that connects these opposites makes sense of what is often today called "both-and thinking" [16]. This phrase is sometimes used just as an excuse for not making up your mind; but very often it refers to this weaving of contrasting perspectives which enables a right decision to be made. This is a case of what we shall later investigate under the name of "context dependent logic". Two opposites can both be true, but not in the same context, and both-and thinking involves using a mediating principle that can take you from one context to another. We will see later in Chapter 8 how this is the sort of logic that emerged as people tried to understand quantum theory in the early 20th century, so that it reflects an aspect of the universe that we have evolved to accommodate in our own thinking.

There is also another case of both-and thinking that occurs in the logic of the deeper levels of our psychology, the levels which, strangely, are involved with both madness and with mystical experience[17]. We will be examining these in Chapter 3. This is an extreme case of these triads where the flow between the opposites and their contexts becomes so complete that there is a paradoxical merging of the two poles into an *inconsistent* logic.

* * * * *** * * * *

I have suggested that the key to humanity's "growing up" is allowing consciousness of this triad to penetrate all areas of our existence. It is already present in our personality and in the cosmos, but we try to close our eyes to this. We often pretend that we can, and should, be perfectly rational, but we cut ourselves off from our bodily awareness of nature on which this rationality has to be based. We approach the material world, including the planet, as if it were an abstract machine governed by totally logical principles, without realising its organic complexity. As a consequence, we suffer and the earth suffers. The situation is repeated in most areas of our culture: a fully integrated flow between opposites eludes us.

This failure of integration is particularly evident in the areas of science and religion which makes it hard for us to grasp how this triad applies. In fact, it operates in two ways: firstly in flowing *between* religion and science, with religion and science corresponding to Eros and Psyche; and secondly, as a connection between intuition and rationality *within* religion and within science. Our failure to understand this human dynamic concerning science and religion is a major impediment to society, because these areas have an enormous hold over human culture. Science, the newcomer, dominates the official thinking of much of the world; while religion continues to be a powerful force in the world, even increasing in many places, but often appearing in horribly distorted forms. The antagonism between science and religion seems to be increasing. Both Christianity, with the rise of opposition to the idea of evolution, and Islam, with the rise of extremist elements, are becoming cut off from their former rational sides. Science reacts to this with the rise of a militant atheism, and both atheism and religion show a tendency to grow increasingly irrational. Integrative wisdom is lacking both within these areas and between them.

Science and religion provide the two most dominant Ways of Knowing: activities through which we form a picture of the world in which we live. While at one time we did this through stories (myths) in which all elements were intertwined, since the time of the hymn to Artemis our major stories have separated out into religion and science, which today have almost no connection with each other. We need to construct a go-between, and the myths I have recounted suggest that the go-between has to do with Nature (Pan). So for our mediating concept, we need a way of understanding Nature, and being in Nature, that connects both with science and religion at the level of culture and knowing. The activity we are looking for is already suggested by the way in which "eco-versions" of many subjects are now emerging: "ecopsychology", "ecospirituality" and so on. We want an eco-mediation. Here I will use the word "Ecology", in a very general sense, for this third culture mediating science and religion. By "Ecology" I do not mean just a branch of science (though that comes into it), but an activity that links science with the beauty and wonder of the world, and thereby moves us to awe and to practical action. This sort of ecology is itself another way of knowing the world.

Knowing:
Science ⟵ ~~Ecology~~ ⟶ Religion

Later on in Chapter 10 I will be looking at how many thinkers and activists are now developing this dynamic sort of ecology under many names: deep ecology, ecopsychology, creation centred spirituality and so on. But first we need to understand both science and religion – quite an undertaking! To begin with I will look at religion, a much misunderstood area. Is it the one source of absolutely certain truth? Or is it a pernicious conspiracy of priests trying to obstruct the liberation brought by science? The fact that both views are at times held shows the need for the third element to hold science and religion together – the element of ecology, of planting in the solid ground of our planet, to bring both these subjects down to earth. It could be said that religion needs science, science needs religion and both need ecology.

3

Belief

Lief: Beloved, dear, agreeable, acceptable, precious (from Aryan
'leubh' – love)

I have suggested that religion needs science, and science needs religion. Each is lame without the other, but together they can create a new way of living on our amazing planet. In this chapter I will start with religion, because it is easy to see the possible connection between religion and ecology. A right religion can restore for us a sense of reverence for the earth, and it can make us integrated within ourselves so that we are able to respond to the call of the earth. Sometimes, however, religion can seem to be doing the opposite of these things. We need to give religion a good hard examination.

So what is religion?

To start with the example of Christianity, my own religion: every Sunday, maybe 200 million people in the world stand up and publicly announce that they "believe in" a number of propositions which, in other circumstances, would seem strange: such as, that Jesus Christ is the son of the creator of the cosmos and that he is "of one substance" with his father – a collection of propositions known in English as the "creed". Is this the essence of religion: affirming collections of controversial statements?

We might try instead to define religion in terms of what people do. Christians go to church on Sundays, Muslims pray five times a day ... and so on. But there are many things that people do in religion: some indigenous people sacrifice animals, some people meditate, some wear special clothes, some eat special food. There are so many different things that people might do as part of their religion that this doesn't really tell us anything.

So instead we might look at "belief" in a deeper sense than just holding to a verbal statement. One can "believe in" someone or something in the sense of trusting in them, in a way that is to do with practical experience rather than theoretical facts. This seems more hopeful. In a lot of religions people "believe in God" in the sense of putting trust in God (the largest single exception is Buddhism) – so this could give us a strong lead as to what religion is. But then we have to think harder about the meaning of "believe" and "God" ... But let us try! At this point I will have to come clean with any strictly traditional Christians who may be still with me by now. While I recognise the historical importance of creeds and scriptures (I will be examining this in the next chapter), what I mean by "religion" is something very different from assenting to particular forms of words and, I will argue, more important.

In the first chapter I suggested that, in Christianity, believing was "undergoing a psychological turning" (which sometimes happened through a conversion experience) . Belief starts from a particular mental orientation, a particular mind-set. In this chapter I want to follow this idea, and show that it can give a reasonable handle on this very diverse thing that we call religion.

If this is where religion starts, in a turning which leads you to put trust in adopting some particular mind-set, then this puts such things as the reciting of the creed (and the intellectual battles that surrounded it, which I will examining in the next chapter) in a different light.

First of all comes belief, a mind-set, and then come statements about God in an attempt to make sense of the belief. The belief itself is a relationship: for Christians, a relationship with the Church, or with an activity in the church, or with Jesus, or with the saints, and so on. Statements come next, as a way of holding on to these relationships. I claim that belief is primarily about "holding dear" the relationships, and not primarily about the statements that express this. Indeed, the word "belief" comes from "lief", an old English word meaning "dear", derived from the same root as the word "love".

But we must go further. Belief has a direction: it is belief "in God", or "in the Teaching", or "in the power of Spirit" – whatever words may be used to express it. Yet it is not the words used that matter, nor is there a specific "thing" that is believed in. It is the quality of the belief that makes for religion, the quality which in the last chapter I associated with awe and sacredness: the sense of something lying beyond ourselves, that gives us a completely different way of knowing the world; a sense that has a quality of power, specialness, or ultra-reality (the numinous).

As I described in the previous chapter, this sense of the sacred is a consequence of the non-verbal parts of our minds, and is essential for being truly human. Though the direction of society in the last few centuries has estranged many of us from this side of our mind and from the numinous side of our experience, its presence still runs throughout life. Some people experience it daily, most people experience it at some time, but modern life tends to push it away into the remote corners of our experience. I suspect that at one time the sense of the sacred was everywhere and it was only after humans started living in cities, and having to obey official authorities in performing humdrum tasks, that a clear distinction emerged between the sacred and its opposite, the boringly secular. In earlier times, and in the oldest cultures today such as that of the aboriginal Australians, there is no clear boundary between what we call religious and what we call secular. People's lives are given meaning and structure by relating them to lots of different stories about the way the world is – stories about the origins of the landscape and the animals, or teaching stories about moral and non-moral behaviour. Some of these stories are linked to practices, such as ritual re-enactments of mythical events in order to ensure the continuing of a safe order in the world. Others are just for telling round the fire in the evening. The whole of life is woven through with the awesome encounters with the numinous. In such societies religion is not something that can be cut out and labelled.

As cultures became more and more town-based, so a distinction emerged between activities and stories that were religious and those that were non-religious, until finally a succession of countries, starting with America[18], even built the separation of religion and non-religion into their legal system, under the principle of "the separation of church and state". In practice, however, there are many modern cultures where religious activities are still so intertwined with practical activities that both seem equally essential parts of the cultural life. This is the case, for instance, with parts of rural Italy and in India, where there is currently a resurgence of religious awareness among the professional classes. It is particularly in North America and Northern Europe where there is a gulf between the sacred and the secular. From these areas has spread what we loosely call "Western culture", whose influence is now felt worldwide.

Science has emerged from this Western culture with its separation of the sacred and the secular. Despite this, science has often been stimulated by the sense of the sacred and the sense of awe that has always filled many scientists, whether astronomers or biologists, so that religious sense and rational analysis have both been present at the birth of many scientific theories. But as these theories have grown up, the prevailing culture has drawn them away from their religious roots. As a result eminent authors such as Stephen Jay Gould and John Polkinghorne have strenuously argued that science and religion are "non-overlapping", both valuable areas and compatible with each other, but dealing with areas that are quite separate. I will argue that the time has now come to bring back a seamless flow between these two areas; but before that we need to explore further into the nature of religion.

*   *   *   *   ****   *   *   *

Religious belief has a direction; it is a belief *in*, or a turning *towards*. I have mentioned that many religions are about belief in God, or in something equivalent to this. The mystical strand of Islam, called Sufism, has a story about the problems of defining "God ".

Three baby fishes, brothers and sisters, were chatting one day about a strange word that they had heard used by some very old fishes. The word was "water". It seemed to have no meaning at all that they could see, so they went to ask their mummy fish what water was. "That is very hard to answer," she replied "but if you can bring me something that is not water, then I will be able to explain what water is."

One moral of the story is that, for someone in a tradition where belief is expressed in terms of God, it is as hard to define "God" as for a fish to define water, and for the same reason: that God is around us, and within us; without it everything that we know would cease to exist.

Another deeper moral is that if you try to define "God" you are missing the point, because any definition makes a distinction between what is God and what is not God; but there is nothing that is not God.

There is a hint here of the idea that conventional logic and reasoning does not hold in religion. On conventional reasoning, anything can be negated, so that if we understand the meaning of "God" then we understand the meaning of "no-God". But if everything is God, then no-God is also God. God is identical with the negation of God, something impossible in conventional logic. We are seeing here the union of opposites that appeared in the mythical character of Artemis in the last chapter.

So the reasoning of the sacred tends to lead to "paradox"; that is, to statements that are both true and false at the same time. The rationalist would say that this means that the notion of God is simply nonsense. But in the realm of the sacred, paradoxes are a hint that you are on the right track. Paradoxes are an example of what is sometimes loosely called "both-and thinking": holding that *both* an idea *and* its negation can be simultaneously valid. We will be looking at this in more detail in the next chapter, and at length when we examine how paradoxes and both-and thinking now are an accepted part of science, and form a vital bridge between science and religion.

Some of the most striking expressions of the paradoxes of God were written in the thirteenth century by the Sufi poet, Rumi, who lived most of his life in what is now Turkey. Many of his poems have been inspired by the words *No God but God!* which form part of the "call to prayer" proclaimed five times a day from the minarets of mosques. Rumi's writings inspired by this saying are full of paradox. For example:

"He said *No God*, then He said *but God*.
No God became *but God*
and Oneness blossomed forth." [19]

Some fifty years later, in what is now Germany, the Christian mystic Eckhart wrote, "I pray God to rid me of God" [20]. For him the concept of God was an obstacle to the reality of God. "God" got in the way of God, because God is not to do with concepts, and so is not governed by the logic of concepts.

I'd like to compare the hints about God (or not-God) that I've just presented with the concept of God given by Richard Dawkins, a well known opponent of religion. In *The God Delusion* he is arguing against "theism" (belief in God), which he defines as follows:

"A theist believes in a supernatural intelligence who, in addition to his main work of creating the universe in the first place, is still around to oversee and influence the subsequent fate of his initial creation. In many theistic belief systems, the deity is intimately involved in human affairs. He answers prayers; forgives or punishes sins; intervenes in the world by performing miracles; frets about good and bad deeds, and knows when we do them (or even think of doing them)." [21]

The God that Dawkins objects to is a petty and factual God. Just the sort of "God" that Eckhart prayed to be rid of. What Dawkins holds up as an argument against religion is in fact an example of what science and religion, at its essential core, have in common: the rejection of the petty God of factual propositions. Dawkins and I agree that humanity is now held back by the petty sort of God that he describes above. But we differ in that I claim that when Dawkins goes on to throw out belief, and throw out the deeper sense of God, he is in fact "throwing the baby out with the bathwater".

But if turning religion into a set of facts is to miss the point, so we equally miss the point if we make religion just a tingly feeling with nothing to do with the actual world. Though we often recognise the sacred by the feeling it gives us, the sacred is just as much part of the world as are facts. We grasp the world, and with it the sacred, through two routes: our reasoning and our intuition, which is linked to our feelings. Just as Western culture has separated religion and science, so it has separated reasoning and intuitive knowing. We have to bring all these together before we can understand religion – and, as we shall be seeing later, before we can truly understand science.

* * * * *** * * * *

Though the essence of religious belief eludes definition, it has two aspects that stand out as hallmarks: unity and love. Unity is the feeling of the oneness of all things, the feeling that you, and all people, and the whole cosmos is absorbed into one whole, which might be named god. Love is the consuming inner passion which not only illuminates the human person, but which the mystics also see as drawing the whole cosmos into completeness. Wholeness looses individual identity in a paradoxical oneness of everything, including opposites. Love mediates between the individual and the whole, drawing the individual to be one with the whole while paradoxically retaining the self. At the end of this chapter, after examining religion, we will see how this dynamic of the individual, love and unity is another reflection of the threefold dynamic of Rationality, Wisdom and Intuition discussed in the last two chapters.

Looking at the world around us today, my references to love and unity in religion might seem bitterly wide of the mark. We regularly hear reports of suicide bomb attacks between Sunni and Shiite Muslims, and conflict between Muslims and Hindus, or between different Christian sects. And all this disunity has continued throughout history with every expression of violence and hatred. This, the opposite of the unity and love that I claim are in fact at the core of religion, is not just an accidental aberration. It is in fact the inevitable transformation of religion into its opposite that takes place when we fail to understand the nature of religion and the nature of human beings. Reaching that understanding is our goal here.

I am convinced that the positive aspects of religions are indispensable if humanity is to flourish, and I will be concentrating on them in the rest of this chapter. I hope to show that the great stream of developing religious belief has, at its core, been towards a greater wisdom and a stronger grasp of positive principles. To this end, I will start with examining Unity.

Unity appears when you discover that the more closely you approach the deepest parts of your experience, the more things come together and seem to be part of a single whole – even thought that whole may be difficult to grasp. One way of thinking about this is in terms of a familiar occurrence: repeatedly, those who experience the natural world as sacred see it something unified. For example, the nineteenth century American essayist Ralph Waldo Emerson wrote of "the Unity of Nature—the Unity in Variety—which meets us everywhere. All the endless variety of things make a unique, an identical impression." [22] I have often experienced things coming together into a greater whole when I am walking in the countryside and find myself "in the flow", in harmony with a world that seems like a single vast organism, of which I am a part, an organism that gently directs me and steers my decisions. Then dogs and butter-flies lead my steps; styles and paths appear just when I need them.

This sort of experience, entirely subjective, is necessarily rather diffuse. It does not explicitly encompass "all the endless variety of things" because these are not presented to us all at once. Rather, it is a general feeling for the unity of what we are encountering at that moment, which then points to the unity of everything. We see this in the writing of John Muir (often regarded as the founder of the environmental movement in the USA) who was launched on his life's work by his first glimpse of the mountain El Capitan in Yosemite. Then he saw that "from the shrubs and half-buried ferns of the floor to the topmost ranks of jewelled pine spires, it is all one finished unit of divine beauty."[23] While it was a particular mountain that inspired him as unity, in his later writing he makes it clear that this sort of unity in diversity belongs to the whole of nature.

Another way of coming to this unity is pragmatic: if you look for unity, you find that things make more sense. This way covers both religious belief and science. Science is dominated by the search for unity, for the one final perfect equation that encapsu-lates the whole of nature. I would be surprised if there were a single master-equation, but the desire to bring phenomena together and see them as aspects of a single system has always proved fruitful and has led to deeper understanding.

Religious unity is revealed when we find ourselves reaching into the depths of nature to grasp that which, so to speak, breathes the sacredness into nature – reaching for something unknown which also, in some religions, breathes sacredness into our own inner experience of our selves.

At this stage I need to make a sharp distinction between unity and uniqueness. Everest is unique in being the highest terrestrial mountain. It is distinguished from all the other mountains. This sort of uniqueness is quite different from the idea of all things hanging together. When religions speak of God as being *one* this does not, in modern religions, mean that God is unique among other gods. It means that the word "God" is shorthand for a unity that embraces everything. As I shall describe shortly, when the religions we know today did start to emerge, they at first *did* think of God as being unique, in the sense of the biggest and best out of all the various demons and spirits that were thought to inhabit the world. But right from the start of human culture the sense of the unity of everything was present alongside this, as we see in the primal religions that are still alive and making an important witness in the lives of the oldest nations today, among the indigenous peoples of America, Asia and Australasia.

In order to give a feel for the way in which the earliest ideas of a unique God grew into the idea of God as an expression of overarching unity, I will give here a quick survey of the way in which this idea of unity has developed. Of course "religion" is such a vast subject that this will be very superficial, and I will only be looking at the strands that led to the organised religions that are numerically dominant today: Hinduism[24], Judaism, Buddhism, Christianity and Islam.

Just as the unity of nature is first grasped in a particular part of nature, and then extended to the whole, so the unity of what lies behind nature, which in the West we call "God", at first emerged as a unity-in-multiplicity of many forms of God. These at first looked like many "gods", but each pointed to a single greater unity lying behind them.

Unity started becoming explicit during the period between 1900 BCE and 1000 BCE. At that time in India the collection of hymns now called the *Rig Veda*, which probably started even earlier, was taking a developed shape. Each hymn uses the names of particular "gods" such as Agni (fire), Indra (water), Varuna (sky, and protector of Order) or Mitra (guardian of friendship and covenants). But the hymns address them in a way that points to the unity of the whole, just as John Muir did when describing El Capitan in the earlier quote. Frequently they couple the names of gods together as if they were just names for the same reality. For example, a hymn to Surya (the Sun) runs:

Homage to the Eye of Mitra and Varuna!
To the mighty God offer this worship
to the farseeing emblem, born of the Gods.
Sing praise to the Sun, the offspring of Heaven.
...
You shine, all living things emerge.
You disappear, they go to rest.
Recognizing your innocence, O golden-haired Sun,
arise; let each day be better than the last.
...
Protect both our species, two-legged and four-legged.
Both food and water for their needs supply.
May they with us increase in stature and strength.
Save us from hurt all our days, O Powers.[25]

Here there are elements of the "big Daddy" aspect of God which Dawkins criticises, and vagueness about whether to refer to many gods or one god or a committee, but these elements are overlain by a sense (which is progressively reinforced by the whole text) of everything being taken up into something greater, symbolised by the sun, but beyond it.

The most famous lines in all the Rig Veda are those that make up the main body of a prayer called the *Gayatri* , still said daily across the world, and used by many other spiritual groups. I have used it in my own prayers for many years, and it is a delight to be able occasionally to go into the local Hindu temple where I live in Southampton and recognise, and join in with, a prayer that has been said by hundreds of millions of people for at least 3000 years, and probably a lot longer. Its text is by now so steeped in resonance that no translation can express it; but from a historical point of view the following gives an idea of the literal meaning of the words (omitting the opening invocation which does not appear with the text in the Rig Veda):

> *O that most longed for, radiance of Savitr,*
> *may we attain your divine glory!*
> *Inspire now our meditation.*

Savitr is another form of the sun god, but the focus is on that which *appears as* the sun, not on the sun itself. Another translation of the opening words *tat savitur varenyam* is "that, the source, worthy of worship". The words all point to elements of unity. *Tat* (that) resonates with later Vedic texts where it is used for what is beyond words; numinosity is expressed in *varenyam* (desired, worthy of worship); and a quality of the ultimate in *savitur* (of Savitr).[26]

While Hinduism continued to develop the idea of many forms of a single "divine" beyond all forms, in the Middle East at the same time there started an alternative approach to unity. The first stage was "monolatry"[27] in which one god was chosen as boss-god and it was decreed that only this god should be worshipped. Then the concept of this god progressively expanded until it embraced a cosmic unity, the religion becoming "monotheism", the belief in a unified god. The event often cited as the origin of monolatry was the reign of the Pharaoh Akhenaten in Egypt. After reigning for a few years during which he followed the religious practices of his ancestors, he abruptly switched to the worship of a single God, Aten, the disk of the Sun. He built a new capital city dedicated solely to Aten, prohibited the worship of any other god, and started to erase from all the statues any names of other gods, and the names of his own ancestors including his father. Not surprisingly (human nature being the same then as now) these changes built up a lot of resentment and were all reversed on his death. But a strand of exclusive monolatry, of worshipping one God with no mention of any rival, seems to have been started by him.

An Egyptian hymn from his reign has verses that are very reminiscent of the hymn to Surya quoted above:

When you set in the western horizon,
Earth falls into a deathly darkness.
People sleep in chambers, heads covered,
Oblivious of the world,
the possessions in their head stolen.
Every lion comes forth from its den,
the serpents sting.
Darkness reigns, earth is silent,
as their maker rests in heavens.

Earth brightens when you rise in the horizon,
when you shine as Aten of daytime.
As you cast your rays,
the Two Lands are in festivity.
Awake, the people are on their feet.
Cleansed and clothed,
their arms adore your appearance.

The entire land sets out to work,
The beasts browse on their herbs,
trees and plants flourish.
The birds fly from their nests,
their wings greeting you,
as the sheep frisk on their feet,
and the insects flutter.
All live when you dawn for them.[28]

The similarities between this and the previous hymn from the Rig Veda has stimulated several attempts to demonstrate a systematic transmission of religion from India to Egypt via Syria. This still remains controversial, however. It could perhaps be a matter of the gradual drift of ideas that were "in the air" for many centuries. What seems more clear cut, however, is the evidence that the exclusive monolatry of Akhenaten was one of the main influences on Judaism, coming as it did in the 14th century BCE, a time that probably coincided with the departure of the Hebrew tribes from Egypt and the birth of the Jewish religion. Indeed, the oldest part of the Hebrew scriptures, the Psalms, contains yet another hymn so similar to part of the Hymn to Aten that it is hard to doubt a direct influence:

You bring darkness, it becomes night,
and all the beasts of the forest prowl
The lions roar for their prey
and seek their food from God.
The sun rises, and they steal away;
they return and lie down in their dens.
Then man goes out to his work,
to his labor until evening.
How many are your works, O Lord!
In wisdom you made them all;
the earth is full of your creatures[29]

From the 14th century BCE on, religion in the Western hemisphere moved towards a more explicit expression of the basic unity that we sense in nature. When we gaze out into the world we first see diversity and then realise a unity underlying it – the unity underlying the unity of nature seen by Emerson and Muir that I started this section with. In Judaism it became expressed in the *shema:* "Hear, O Israel: the Lord our God is one Lord"[30], which was incorporated into Christianity and was in turn to inspire the Islamic *shahada (No God but God!)* already quoted.

Meanwhile, in India a different approach to unity was gradually unfolding. Around the 8th century BCE[31] the first of the scriptures known as the Brahmanas were composed, followed by the more developed Upanishads. Rather than the hymns of praise and worship that marked the much earlier Rig Veda, these were infused by a spirit of interior contemplation and unity. The Upanishads contained teaching material, often couched in the form of a story, about spiritual knowing.

Here are some extracts from one of the most influential passages of the Chandogya Upanishad, one of the earliest to be composed. The teacher Uddalaka Aruni is talking to his son, Svetaketu. He begins by describing what is going on during the basic Hindu practice of meditation, in which one focuses on one's breathing. Then, a little later, he extends the picture to the ultimate goal of mind, which is the realisation of unity:

"As a bird when tied by a string flies first in every direction, and finding no rest anywhere, settles down at last on the very place where it is fastened, exactly in the same manner, my son, that mind[32] after flying in every direction, and finding no rest anywhere, settles down on breath; for indeed, my son, mind is fastened to breath."

"... When a man departs from hence, his speech is merged in his mind, his mind in his breath, his breath in heat (fire), heat in the Highest Being.

Now that which is that subtle essence (the root of all), in it all that exists has its self. It is the True. It is the Self, and thou, O Svetaketu, art it."[33]

The final sentence contains the famous words *tat tvam asi* – "that art thou" – which are constantly reiterated later in the text. In the many centuries since the early Rig Veda we have passed from *tat savitur varenyam* (that source, worthy of worship) to *tat tvam asi* (that art thou). During this time radical changes have taken place within human experience. It has become richer. The spiritual technology of meditation has been developed, as alluded to in these verses, and as a result a whole inner world of experience has opened up, a world of equal wonder to the outer world. So, by the time of the Upanishads, experience has come to involve a greater diversity: on one hand are the many aspects of vividness and wonder in the natural world, on the other hand are the many shades of powerful and mysterious experiences of the inner world. The idea of unity-in-diversity has intensified, both the sense of unity and the sense of diversity becoming deeper. The inner feeling of numinosity, of overwhelming reality, has come to be seen as the same as the feeling of power experienced in the outer world. It is the same "that" (*tat*) which is seen in each, so that unity is rediscovered on different levels.

The inner, termed *Atman*, was developed, as was the outer, termed *Brahman*. And in another Upanishad, often regarded as of equal age to, or older than the Chandogya, we find the explicit statement or this ultimate unity: *this Atman is Brahman, it is made of everything*[34].

To recap this historical sketch: earliest religion was a seamless unity of outer engagement, trained observation, mental reflection, dreams, imagination, trance, visions and so on. By the late 9th century BCE it had been separated out into the inner and the outer. This dynamic of separation and unification threads through religion and culture from the first millennium BCE onwards. In the time of the Upanishads the web of existence was diversified but unbroken, and through subsequent developments the role of unity never disappeared from sight.

From the 15th and 16th centuries in Europe, however, the unity seemed progressively to fall apart. Human culture separated out into the sacred and the secular, just as intuition and reason have separated out, leading to the dilemmas of the present day. So now there is a need to bring back essential unity; to bring back "that", which is both the glory of the rising sun and the "soul" of the boy Svetaketu.

Of course, such a sketch is absurdly oversimplified. The history of religion is perhaps the most vast and complex subject that can be imagined, and we could wander forever in the different forms taken by the idea of unity. Later in this book I will be narrowing the focus to Christianity, the religion with greatest influence on early science in Europe, when these ideas can be more carefully explored.

Before moving on to this, however, I will finish our discussion of unity with an important contribution from the Buddhist tradition, and then explore the second hallmark of belief: love.

* * * * *** * * * *

I have already mentioned that belief in God is not a part of Buddhism. It is as much a philosophy of life as a religion, and so is a rather different case from the religions we have been looking at. It does unity differently, and we can learn from this.

Within Buddhist experience and teaching, the world is not seen as a collection of well-defined objects, like pieces of furniture on a stage, but as a place of continual flux and change. The person, "I", is not a fixed being, but more like a very persistent eddy in a stream (persisting, in fact over many lifetimes). People, rocks, trees ... are happenings within a flow:

they come to be and they pass away.

But the coming-to-be, the arising of a being or a quality, is not a random event, nor is it produced by a God "up there". Each arising is determined by a relationship with all the other arisings around it. This is called *dependent co-arising*. The Vietnamese Buddhist teacher Thich Nhat Hanh uses the more attractive term *interbeing* for this, which he explains as the way in which "things do not exist separately and outside each other. In reality, things exist inside each other and with each other."[35] So a happening *A* occurs as a result of its relationship with *B, C, D* ... around it, and *B* happens because of *A, C, D* ... and so on. Everything is in relation to everything else.

There is a story about this, derived from a Buddhist text called the Avatamsaka Sutra about the "Web of Indra". This sutra (scripture) seems to have been re-translated and re-told so often that its original has disappeared from view. Here is a modern version by Francis Cook

"Far away in the heavenly abode of the great god Indra, there is a wonderful net which has been hung by some cunning artificer in such a manner that it stretches out indefinitely in all directions. In accordance with the extravagant tastes of deities, the artificer has hung a single glittering jewel at the net's every node, and since the net itself is infinite in dimension, the jewels are infinite in number. There hang the jewels, glittering like stars of the first magnitude, a wonderful sight to behold. If we now arbitrarily select one of these jewels for inspection and look closely at it, we will discover that in its polished surface there are reflected all the other jewels in the net, infinite in number. Not only that, but each of the jewels reflected in this one jewel is also reflecting all the other jewels, so that the process of reflection is infinite."[36]

This is an extraordinary expression of unity. Not only are we and all things linked together, as in a net, but we are in such a close dynamic relationship with everything else that they are a part of us and we are a part of them. The world is linked into a great vibrating whole through mutual relationship.

This interrelationship has profound moral consequences. If everything is part of me, then it surely is inevitable that I will love them "as myself". As Joanna Macy puts it:

"Now we see that everything we do impinges on all beings. The way you are with your child is a political act, and the products you buy and your efforts to recycle are part of it too. So is meditation—just trying to stay aware is a task of tremendous importance. We are trying to be present to ourselves and each other in a way that can save our planet. Saving life on this planet includes developing a strong, caring connection with future generations; for, in the Dharma [cosmic law] of co-arising, we are here to sustain one another over great distances of space and time.

The Dharma wheel, as it turns now, also tells us this: that we don't have to invent or construct our connections. They already exist. We already and indissolubly belong to each other, for this is the nature of life. So, even in our haste and hurry and occasional discouragement, we belong to each other. We can rest in that knowing, and stop and breathe, and let that breath connect us with the still center of the turning wheel."[37]

So the Buddhist version of unity, far from being more abstract, takes us straight to the planetary crisis of the previous chapter, to saving life on the planet, and offers the encouragement that we can engage with this in simple practical ways.

* * * * *** * * * *

The second hallmark aspect of belief is love, a word that lies at the origin of the word "belief". Love is prominent in every major religion, though its flavour varies from one religion to another, and the actual word used varies. Love is more prominent in the "Abrahamic religions" (Judaism, Christianity and Islam) than in the religions of the East.

Christianity stresses love more than any other religion. In Christian scripture love is the essence of God (so that "John" can write "God is love"[38]) and love is the essence of worship, belief and community. The core of the original Christian church was the community of love as initiated by Jesus with his disciples. It was a divine love, carrying the characteristic qualities of sacredness that we have already noted, filled with a divine power. The Apostle Paul describes this quality in one of the most famous passages of Christian Scripture:

"Love is patient, love is kind. It does not envy, it does not boast, it is not proud. It is not rude, it is not self-seeking, it is not easily angered, it keeps no record of wrongs. Love does not delight in evil but rejoices with the truth. It always protects, always trusts, always hopes, always perseveres. Love never fails."[39]

Judaism and Islam take a more cautious approach than Christianity. For one thing, they use different terms for referring to God's love for the world, our love for God and our love for each other. Love still has a strong place, but it is more qualified.

In Islam, like Christianity, love is affirmed as the prime attribute of God. Every chapter of the Qur'an begins with the words *Bismillah ir-rahman ir-rahim* "(I begin) with the name of God, most gracious most compassionate". The word "compassion" sounds rather detached, and the word "gracious" rather legalistic. But the true resonances of the words can be seen from their derivation. Arabic, like other Semitic languages such as Hebrew and Aramaic, is based on a small number of *roots*, clusters of consonants, which are developed into a variety of words and grammatical forms by the addition of vowels and modification of the consonants. In normal writing only the consonants are written (the vowels are implied by the context) and so all the reader usually sees are the roots. The words *rahman* and *rahim* for "the gracious" and "the compassionate" both come from the one root RHM whose basic meaning is "womb"; they derive, that is, from the physical bond between a mother and her child, perhaps the most fundamental form of love.

Exactly the same situation holds with the Hebrew scriptures, where the word for "compassionate" is *raham*, derived from the same root, and used in phrases such as "Thou, O Lord art a God full of compassion"[40]. So in both Judaism and Islam the love that God has for the world is the love of a Mother for her child. And in Islam this love encompasses the whole of God's aspects, because it is held that the whole of the Qur'an is contained in these opening words.

Judaism, in particular, then moves on from an acceptance of God's love for humanity, to considering how this determines humanity's attitude to God. The key biblical text here is the *shema*, cited earlier, which continues "thou shalt love the Lord thy God with all thine heart, and with all thy soul, and with all thy might". Love flows both ways, from God to humans and from humans to God.

An interesting feature, however, is that the Hebrew scriptures use a different word (*ahab*) for the "love" of humans for God, from the word *raham* used in the case of the love of God for humans. The distinction is yet more complex in Islam. We find verses of the Qur'an which use the same word for the two direction love between humans and God, such as "Say [O prophet]: 'If you love God follow me, [and] God will love you and forgive you of your sins."[41] – using the same word (*tuhib*) in both cases. But it is a different word from *rahim*, which refers to

54

the essential love that constitutes the being of God.

Other qualities such as service, charity, faithfulness and forbearance are often placed above love, perhaps reflecting the practical tone of the Qur'an and the sayings, which often address the realities of 7th century society.

Alongside this, however, runs the mystical side of Islam, Sufism, which is completely focused on passionate love for God. Here is another quotation from Rumi, whose verses always circle the theme of humanity's love for God:

Whoever sees thy face
will never go to a rosegarden;
whoever tastes thy lips
will never talk of wine.
When thy tresses sweep the air
musk withholds its fragrance;
in the light of your face,
every thought turns aside.[42]

Though Buddhism does not focus on God, we still find love as a dominant theme, in the form of compassion *(metta)* — or "loving kindness" as the word is often translated. The chief attribute of the Buddha is compassion, and the basic work of the Buddhist is to extend compassion to all beings through action and meditation. Interestingly, the Buddhist concept of *sangha* (spiritual community) has many parallels with the role of the Christian church-group: a group resting in a single group-mind in which the individuals can find a combination of freedom, inspiration and tuition. Buddhists speak of the three jewels of refuge: "I take refuge in the Buddha. I take refuge in the *dharma* [cosmic law or teaching]. I take refuge in the *sangha* [spiritual community]." Many Christians could echo this confession of love in terms of the Christ-mind, Holy Wisdom, and the Church.

Hinduism is perhaps the only major religion in which love is not absolutely predominant, at least in relation to God. Instead, love is recognised as one path to the divine, the path of devotion *(bhakti)*. The other major path to God is the path of wisdom *(jñani)*. One characteristic of Hiduism is its feeling for balance in the universe: the wise person recognises that there is no shying away from the presence of darkness and suffering.

* * * * *** * * *

But what about morality? Surely religion must include (to go back to Dawkins) a God who "forgives or punishes sins"? And is not this the straightforward answer to questions about the environment: despoiling God's creation is a sin against the creator? So the way ahead is to accept our moral duty and get on with obeying God. Which would make most of this book super-fluous.

Morality – how you behave in society– is an integral part of being human. From the first moment when the baby starts to feel a distinction between "I" and "Thou", to a person's establishment as head of a family or tribe, the human being is weaving her life as part of the weft of social morality. So, in the stories told round the fire in cultures when religion, science and law were one seamless whole, there was no separation between "what you ought" and "what is". Stories told by the elders were a way of teaching morality to the younger members of the community, at the same time as teaching what the universe was like. I have described, however, how these different strands progressively separated and religion, as it developed, took on a character of its own.

I have also described how this emergence of religion had different characters in different continents, which has resulted in different relations between religion and morality. For Judaism, whose focus has been described by Sayed Hussein Nasr as lifting the community into the divine, morality and religion are inextricable. The core scripture (the first five books of the Bible) is called the *Torah*, which means "law". Judaism is founded on the notion of a covenant between humanity and God, which on the human side took the form of sacred law. Any approach to God has to be on a basis of obedience to the law of God, who was in the older scriptures presented as the ultimate Father-figure giving moral commandments to the subordinate young. Similarly Islam, which fully recognises the divine character of the *Torah*, has from its inception stressed that the moral law implications of the Qur'an and the sayings of the Prophet are an integral part of the revelation of Islam. Here, however, moral law is presented as something integral to the created world order, rather than a command handed out arbitrarily by a Father-God.

In the East, where the idea of laws given by a personal God was not a strong influence, the emphasis was also on morality as part of the intrinsic law of the universe, in this case the law of "action" (*karma*). Acting against the moral grain of the universe would result in your being reincarnated at an inferior level, and therefore you were motivated to behave morally in order to flourish in the next life. This belief has never, as far as I know, resulted in an attempt to deduce a specific moral code from the law of Karma – perhaps because of the lack of sufficiently consistent data concerning what acts led to which reincarnations.

Christianity, while it arose from Judaism, very characteristically places love above moral law. Jesus is presented as teaching that the principle of love, illustrated by forgiving your enemy time after time and "turning the other cheek" to those who slap you, fulfils Jewish law and then goes beyond it. The apostle Paul wrote: "Owe no man any thing, but to love one another: for he that loves another has fulfilled the law". While Judaism taught that first one had to achieve moral purity, and then one could approach God, Christianity taught that first you had to love God, and then from that would follow love of neighbour and self, and from that would follow moral behaviour. (Of course, one can question whether this actually works in practice.) Similarly in Buddhism morality follows from the fundamental principle of universal compassion.

So we have a roughly historical progression from story and commands by a Father-figure, to a concept of law as part of the cosmos, and then to a justification for law in terms of a higher principle of love/compassion. The more religious thought penetrates to fundamental principles, the more this understanding seems to resonate with some sort of desire for "rightness" in the universe. A fixed moral code can behave in ways that seem monstrous when a new situation arises, or when people put moral rules above common sense kindness. Worse, rules that a tribe introduces as a ritual element, such a prohibitions on homosexuality, can become mixed up with moral laws or even given a higher status than the law of love.

As we have already seen, this development of the notion of morality and love in the way humanity relates to God, and hence to each other, was reflected in notions about how God relates to humans. The key transition, expressed explicitly in Christianity and Buddhism, but implicit in important strands within other religions, is from morality to love. That is, from the God of Dawkins, who issues commands and punishes those who disobey, to the God of, for example, the Christian Scriptures who, according to the author of the Letters of John, "*is* love" and who calls us to love in return.

Within all theistic religions there is still a tension between morality and love, but it is particularly present in Islam because the Qur'an has, on a superficial reading, a greater emphasis than other scriptures on the afterlife, where people either experience happiness or pain as a necessary consequence of their actions in this life. This has lead some Islamic mystics, with their emphasis on love as opposed to seeking rewards, to protest against an overemphasis on the afterlife. They saw this superficial reading of scripture as a "veil" that could hide us from the reality of God.

The Sufi saint Rabi'a al-Adawiya of Basra expressed this principle in all her life. She once walked through the streets holding a flaming torch in one hand and a bucket of water in the other. When asked what she was doing she replied, "I want to set fire to paradise and to pour water over hell, so that these two veils disappear and it becomes plain who venerates God for love and not for fear of hell or hope for paradise." She prayed for love, not Grace:

"O my Lord, if I worship Thee from fear of Hell, burn me in Hell, and if I worship Thee in hope of Paradise, exclude me thence, but if I worship Thee for Thine own sake, then withhold not from me Thine Eternal Beauty."[44]

Though they can be a bit exhausting, we need more Rabi'as in the world today, who are not afraid to respond to love with love in return, not asking what we can get out of it.

But – and this is a most vital "but" – there is nothing simple or easy about love. We do not enter a calm sea of plain sailing when we pass from morality to love. On the contrary, we may enter stormier seas, buffeted by emotions, where logic often seems powerless, and intuition provides an uncertain compass. Love is not being nice to people; it operates at a much deeper level. The God who is Love is also the God of the earthquake, and this baffles logic. So we must now probe deeper into just what this strange quality is.

*   *   * * *** *   *   *   *

Granted that something related to "love" is involved in most religion, do we really know what "love" is? The word in English alone can mean many things: maternal love (in all its forms, whether caring or possessive), sexual love, which can shade into aggression, compassionate love that strives to move to be beside the suffering and the dispossessed and help in their struggles, communal love that flows through a group animating them and empowering them, devotional love that yearns for the unattainable heights of the divine, and so on. Do these have anything at all in common? If not, perhaps it would be better to use some more restricted word like compassion or devotion.

In a previous book I have argued that there is in fact something quite specific working at large in the universe, which we can identify as the love that is referred to in religions, and which we can regard as "love-proper". The other forms of love can then be seen as modifications of this. I will summarise and update this argument now.

All human emotions tend to be mixed, involving all our bodies, our conscious thoughts and our unconscious motivations in various mixtures. Nothing will be found in an unmixed form. But we can nonetheless distinguish theoretically the distinct elements involved in various forms of love, even though they are never found pure and alone. Recognising this, we can first separate out narrow biological appetites, particularly, in the case of love, the drive built into us for reproduction. After we have, so to speak, bracketed off this and other such drives, we are left with the core of love, something which is still a basic part of being human, and may be genetically conditioned, but which is not a drive towards a specific biological function (though of course we would expect it to have played a general role in our evolution).

Its characteristics were expressed by Scott Peck in his definition of love as "The will to extend one's self for the purposes of nurturing one's own or another's spiritual growth." Unlike some forms of sexual desire, it has nothing to do with taking something in order to gratify oneself: it is extending oneself, usually for the benefit of another. Neither is it grace (in the narrower sense of the last section), the showering of gifts dispassionately, at arm's length, with no actual movement in oneself. Rather, in love for another I extend and give of myself. And in the more mysterious love that I feel for the wholeness of things, and for what draws me into this wholeness — what in traditional language is called love for God — I find myself opened up and enlarged, and I myself grow spiritually as a result. If the phrase "for the purposes of nurturing one's own or another's spiritual growth" still slightly smacks of doing something in order to get something in return, we could perhaps rephrase Scott Peck's definition as "The will to extend one's self in response to a desire for the nurturing of a common spiritual growth."

Looked at more closely, love is the desire to enter into and participate in a greater whole, or a delight in doing so. The "participation" is not a losing of oneself, not a dying into the greater whole (at least not in the initial stages) but a state of both acting as an individual self and also, at the same time, being received into something greater and acting creatively as an element in it. That whole acts through me, but as a part of my own action. It is another example of the paradoxical both-and thinking of the realm of the sacred: both my free action and the free action of the greater. We can see how this desire and delight enters into many of the senses of love we have looked at. Sexual love is driven by a specific appetite, but in humans it is most fulfilling when it is joined with the desire to form "an item" – a greater whole with a life of its own from which each partner draws fulfilment and from which far more creativity flows than would be possible from the individuals alone. We can see from our pets that this is not restricted to humans: we might speculate that in mammals generally, if not more widely, the same is true. The same principle can hold for the collective mind of a group, as in the case of the Christian church or the Buddhist *sangha*. One might almost say the essence of life is this formation of collective wholes — trees in the forest, cells in the body, "organelles" that were once bacteria in the cells and so on. The universe is knit together by this tendency, which appears to consciousness as love and to physics as particular emergent processes. So we can truly echo the closing line of Dante's *Divine Comedy*: "the love that moves the Sun and the other Stars".

Consciously entering into this process of love, which fulfils and enlarges the self, always carries to some extent the feeling of numinosity, and so is always sacred. That is not to say that the act we might be doing at the time is "right", in the sense of harmonising with yet wider levels of love and greater wholes. The Nazi rallies at Nuremberg carried this numinous charge, and from the film footage of Hitler's tours through Germany there can be no doubt that a great many people were moved by a real love for him. But this love was placed at the service of destruction and disharmony. It lacked discernment. We recall that belief, the entry into the sacred, is not just a feeling, but a combination of feeling and discernment, as we are seeking in this book.

We can see now that unity and love, the two hallmarks of belief, are in fact not two separate qualities, but different aspects of the same thing: love is the longing for being taken up into a greater whole, and the result of this process of building greater wholes is unity — a unity in diversity. When love is seen in this way, we realise that it flows in both directions: I as an individual long for a greater context — I celebrate the love between me and my partner, and beyond this I am drawn in love for the earth, echoing the idea of an "upward" love of humanity for "God". And at the same I receive nourishment and blessing from the flourishing of the partnership or of the earth, echoing the "downward" love (compassion) of "God" for humanity.

But this giving and receiving is not just a transaction between two separate individuals. When I suggested above that love was about a "common spiritual growth" I had in mind the way in which I feel that I am a part of a greater whole, and I feel in myself the growth of the whole and the delight of the whole. My boundaries start to melt so that it is not that I love and I am being loved, but that I am taken up into this delight that is greater than

myself. Love is thus not a receiving, or a giving, but a participation in a circulating two-way flow, which in a previous book I
called "the double breath of love".

If we need a definition of religion, therefore, perhaps the
closest we can get is "willed and discerning participation in the
mutual love of the greatest whole".

At the end of this survey of belief, we therefore find, in the
flow of love, a reflection within of the triad introduced in the
previous chapter:

Religion:

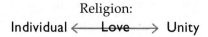

Individual ⟵———Love———⟶ Unity

4

Councils

Council: (from Latin con- together + cal- to call) a convocation, assembly, meeting, union

I now want to look at the connections and the differences between religion and that other dominating social force, Science.

In the year 325 CE the Emperor Constantine I convened a gathering of the bishops of the Christian Church at Nicaea (now the town of İznik in Turkey). About 300 bishops or their delegates attended, accompanied by support staff — over 1000 people from a region stretching round the entire Mediterranean, from Spain to Palestine to Libya. After discussing for a month some of the most intricate philosophical ideas ever formulated, decisions were taken which (following much subsequent and often violent ideological conflict) fixed the creed of the church to this day — despite objections from supporters of the theologian Arius, who held that Jesus was not 'of one substance with the Father'. This gathering is known as the First Council of Nicaea.

In the year 1927 CE the trustees of the fund instituted by the Industrialist Ernest Solvay convened a gathering of physicists at the city of Brussels, in Belgium. About 29 physicists attended, of whom 17 were or became Nobel Prize winners. After discussing for 6 days some of the most intricate scientific ideas ever formulated, a general consensus emerged which (following much subsequent and usually friendly debate) fixed the modern theory of quantum mechanics, despite Einstein's contention that 'God does not play dice'. This gathering is known as the Fifth Solvay Conference.

Both gatherings took place at pivotal moments in the history of Europe (and, for 1927, of the world) and they reflected the character of these moments. Constantine was aware of the importance of controlling spiritual power, as well as military and economic power, and he was a shrewd assessor of all three. A Christian himself, he backed the Church, which had previously been persecuted, and tried to ensure that it was strongly organised and integrated within his Empire. This laid foundations for the structure of Europe that would be influential for the next thousand years and beyond. The Council of Nicaea was thus dedicated to trying to build a united church that could promulgate the clear and powerful message that, to put the outcome simply, Jesus is God.

Ernest Solvay had invented a revolutionary process for manufacturing sodium carbonate (the basis of a whole range of industrial products) far more efficiently than hitherto, and had become wealthy as a result. He put his wealth into educational foundations that were characteristic of the new culture that we now call "modernity", a culture based on the intensive application of science and scientific principles. He inaugurated an Institute for Sociology, a Business School and Foundations for Physics and Chemistry.

I have chosen here two moments which were crucial for the Christian religion and for science. In this chapter I will examine these as examples of the power and excitement of both religion and science, and as examples of the problems that beset both of them. We will start to see how, despite their obvious differences, the conferences have remarkable similarities, and fit together in a most surprising way. Together they hint at a new glimpse of reality; a glimpse that if realised and translated into living would enable us to care joyfully for the earth.

*   *   *   *   ***   *   *   *   *

The Council of Nicaea was a notoriously bad-tempered affair, illustrating the "fanaticism" which, for many people today, expresses all that is wrong with religion. Different factions, stirred up by political intrigue, were defending different and, from our modern perspective, apparently arbitrary interpretations of the Bible. It may be helpful to recap how Christianity had got into this situation through its development over the preceding three centuries.

The basis for Christianity lay in the many accounts of Jesus' life and sayings, which were circulating in the first hundred years or so after his death. As the early church tried to consolidate its power and present a consistent message, the original wide range of documents was whittled down, alternatives being banned and burnt, leaving by the fourth century those we now have in the Bible: the accounts of Jesus in the Gospels, the Acts of the Apostles and in parts of the letters of Paul[45]. Only a dozen or so partial copies — such as the gospel of Mary, and the more substantial two gospels of Thomas — remind us of the range that once existed.

The surviving documents presented a picture of Jesus, a charismatic healer and teacher who referred to God as "Father", and also as "your Father" when addressing his disciples. Following his death and reported resurrection he was felt as an intangible presence in the meetings of the early Church, a presence which they called "the Holy Spirit". This experience, and the subsequent vision of Jesus which came to Paul, moved the church to start regarding Jesus as divine and in some sense "the Son of God". Thus the early church found itself speaking of "The Father", "The Son" and "The Holy Spirit".

The question then naturally arose as to what the relation between these entities really was. Was Jesus a lesser God, or an aspect of the one God of Judaism, or a superior angel, or a super-human? If Jesus had the power to give Christians an eternal life in heaven after death, as was suggested in many of the versions of his teaching, then he must have a rank almost as high as God. On the other hand he died a very human and ignominious death, and many of his sayings seemed to suggest that Jesus regarded "The Father" as far higher than himself, suggesting more that he was some kind of advanced human who achieved divine status as a result of his faithfulness and suffering.

Religious politics complicated the issue. Christianity was competing for supporters with the state religion of the Roman Gods, as well as with Judaism and a variety of minor sects. Christianity needed to define its superiority to these. Its unique selling point was the promise of eternal life through belief in Jesus, a god-man to whom believers could relate in an intimate way. Jesus was "seated at the right hand of the Father" in order to make sure that the believer was well received in heaven, thus acting as a guarantee of eternal life. If Jesus was just a man, the promise of eternal life was much less convincing. On the other hand if Jesus, the Father and the Holy Spirit were three separate gods, then Christianity started to look like the same sort of tired polytheism as the Roman state religion and so lost its appeal. Get it right, and Christianity would become powerful and could negotiate a working relationship with the Emperor; get it wrong and Christianity would be seen as competition that was weak enough to be eliminated by persecution.

There was a need for a simple message with which to rally the faithful and convert people from other religions, but it was very hard to fit in all the elements that were needed. One big problem was; what was the meaning of the world "Son" in relation to Jesus? By definition the word implies that Jesus had to be "begotten" by the Father. But whereas there was no problem with gods and goddesses "begetting" in the lusty Greek and Roman religion, the idea of begetting by the usual method would be both impious and a philosophical blunder in Christianity. Their God was the transcendent God of Judaic monotheism who was supposed to be totally unchangeable.

Prior to the Council of Nicaea, the theologian Arius put forward a fairly rational proposal for sorting this out. The "begetting" of the Son was really a "creation", essentially the same sort of thing as the way God had created the universe out of nothing. The Son was first created on a separate spiritual plane, then subsequently, Jesus entered the world through Mary. Arius actually put it more subtly than this, so as not to frighten off those who wanted a totally divine Son, but this was the sort of picture that his followers probably took from his teaching.

Against this, the conservative faction, led by Athanasius, took the bull by the horns and promoted a solution that was a straight paradox. The Father was God, the Son was also God, they had the same powers and properties and so were essentially the same God, but they were two, not one, so that the Son could become man while the Father remained in heaven. Take it or leave it and never mind the contradictions. The problem of the Holy Spirit was deferred to a later date.

There was something of a Greek-Roman split involved in the difference between Arius and Athanasius. The Western, Latin speaking branch of the church to which Athanasius belonged, based on the now rather run-down city of Rome, regarded it reasonable to declare that the Father and the Son were both the same and different, because they said so; whereas the Eastern, Greek speaking branch, based on cities such as Antioch, Nicomedia and Alexandria, insisted that any solution had to be rational and coherent if was to be sold to their more sophisticated population.

The debate took some 60 years to reach a conclusion. Athanasius won the first round at Nicaea, but this was followed by a succession of further Councils convened by the supporters of both sides at intervals of 1 to 5 years. The dispute was carried out not only through debate, but also through civil wars, assassinations, riots, kidnapping, excommunications and banishments. The conclusion was finally reached as a result of the progressive weakening of the Roman Empire by external attacks and through a triumph of Greek subtlety devised by Gregory of Nyssa and his colleagues, which enabled all parties to interpret the wording of the resolution in the way that they wanted.

The basic idea of the solution was to analyse what was meant when we talk about things being "the same". As an example of one meaning, imagine yourself in a train and noticing that you are reading "the same book" as the person opposite. When you say "the same" in this case you do not mean that the person opposite is leaning across and literally reading your book; you mean that the books are *essentially* the same, from the point of view of what makes a book what it is. Gregory, like Athanasius before him, proposed that The Son and the The Father were the same in this sense. They shared the same *essence* (the Greek word was *ousia*).

This dealt with the "same" part of problem. The new trick introduced by Gregory of Nyssa was to refine the sense in which the Father and the Son were *different*. This is easy in the case of the two books in the train: they are different in many ways — being made of different batches of paper, and being in different places, for example. But these differences were of no use when applied to God (or Gods): God was not made out of a particular batch of matter, and did not have a place. In order to express this, Gregory proposed that they had different *hypostases*. This Greek word, which had also been applied to the problem by others before him, means the constant factor that "stands under" a change of quality or nature. For example, when water changes into ice, we might say (very pompously) that the same *hypostasis* is involved in each, but the nature of ice is different from the nature of water[46]. By developing this term Gregory was able to develop a picture of Jesus as different from the Father in that he could have a human nature, whereas the Father couldn't. In this way we could relate to Jesus as truly one of us; but he was the same as God in his power and status.

*   *   * * *** *   *   *   *

What is important here is not so much the tortuous details of what was agreed, which to most of us today seems very far-fetched, but the dynamics surrounding how it was agreed, principally as regards the interplay between rationality and intuitive knowing.

On the intuitive side, all involved had a deep intuitive conviction of the rightness and importance of their basic starting points. Christianity *mattered*. In the late Roman Empire life was tough for most people, whether struggling to retain enough grain for their own use in the face of rising grain-taxes, or fighting battles on the frontiers. Eternal bliss afterwards in heaven was not to be sneezed at. It was a debate that struck to the heart of every person's most basic fears and desires, to their very identity. Every move was thus charged with high emotion. The theological issues were also filled with that hallmark of the divine that I have already identified: sacredness, awe, numinosity, which ratcheted up the emotional tone and gave it the particular quality of all religious experience.

Those pursuing the rational side of human responses pulled out all the stops to try to match the emotional weight of the intuitive side, but rationality was ultimately inadequate to the task. Words fail in the face of deep emotion and deep intuitive knowing, both of which were here combined. The intellectual formula reached tried to match with its complexity what intuitive knowledge delivered with its intensity. Words were finally found to patch up the problem, but words only point to what is beyond them. This is the constant dynamic of human life. We become hopelessly lost unless we remain aware of this dynamic and sensitive to it — unless we open ourselves to the flow that connects them. As we have seen, in religion this is the flow of love, which was conspicuously lacking from most of the partici-pants in the early church councils.

At Nicaea and the subsequent councils, attempts at rational verbal solutions were repeatedly swept away by fear and passion. As the centuries passed the church responded to this challenge by trying to enforce the rational dogmatic side of religion more and more, ignoring love and brutally enforcing adherence to rational theology. This tragic history poses one of the greatest obstacles to integrating science and religion in the West; and the clue to removing this obstacle lies in that other conference in 1927.

* * * * *** * * * *

Just as the delegates at the Council of Nicaea were passionate about the power of Jesus, so the delegates at the fifth Solvay conference, which I will describe later, were intuitively and passionately convinced of the power of the scientific method. From then on, civilisation could move forward, founded on a true knowledge based on solid, objective experimentation. But some investigators of quantum theory were proposing that the world had uncertainty at its heart; and that the "observer" might influence the outcomes of experiments. With all this uncertainty, science might lose its power to save humanity. Such views were felt as a threat to the certainty and objectivity of the scientific method, and a real danger to modern rationality.

For both gatherings, the defence against these dangers was seen to lie in getting clear rational statements of what the situation really was. What made agreement difficult was the numinous power of the intuitive component. At Nicaea the intuitive component was the fundamental stuff of religion, the encounter with the numinous. At Solvay the intuitive side was more subtle, and was expressed in the discussions between the two most eminent participants: Albert Einstein and Niels Bohr.

While all creative work involves intuition in an essential way, for Einstein intuitive and aesthetic criteria were explicit. For him, the ultimate physical laws had to be clear and beautiful. He would often express this by referring to "God", perhaps only as a figure of speech, in phrases such as "God is subtle but not malicious". Also he claimed that the "mystical" was a vital part of being human. Bohr, on the other hand, was a pragmatist. He was equally determined to uncover the basic laws of the universe, but he looked for guidance to the established practices of physicists in their laboratories rather than to the intrinsic beauty of the principles. So Bohr insisted that physics had to retain its basic concepts like energy, mass and momentum because without these communication between physicists would be impossible; whereas Einstein believed that a new physics called for new concepts.

By emphasising the actual practices of physicists, Bohr was led to a theory in which traditional concepts could still be used, but only within precisely defined limits. One was, for instance, allowed to use the concept of "position" when referring to the outcome of a laboratory measurement, but not when referring to a tiny particle. In many circumstances there seemed to be no rational cause for why one experimental outcome appeared rather than another, and here Bohr insisted that it was a matter of "randomness". For Einstein this was impossibly inaesthetic: in discussions at Solvay he insisted that "God does not play dice".

Einstein repeatedly raised ingenious challenges to Bohr's views, and Bohr with equal ingenuity refuted each one of them. Bohr and his supporters were producing a usable theory, albeit a very strange one, while Einstein has no detailed alternative to offer. We might speculate how history might have been otherwise if, at that point, Einstein had carried the argument and started a different theory based on new concepts with stronger spiritual implications. But this did not happen, and quantum theory was set to evolve along the firmly rationalistic lines laid down by Bohr, as I shall describe later. The principle that concepts had precise limits to their applicability, beyond which physical behaviour became random, proved immensely fruitful, giving rise to the whole science of atomic physics and particle physics, and to all the technological applications, from electron microscopes to transistors, that are so vital to us today. Only now are we starting to realise that there is an alternative, more intuitional aspect of nature, which we now need to recover in order to flourish on our planet. Perhaps Einstein was glimpsing this at the Solvay conference, but had no way of formulating it.

As I compose these words, a nearly full moon rises above the trees ahead of me into a glowing pinky-grey sky, pierced by the darting black shapes of squealing swifts. Nicaea and Solvay alike would deny any ultimate reality to this ravishing vision, as compared to the bliss of heaven or the objectivity of physical equations. And yet for us humans, if the beauty of this evening sky is not real, what is? Here is the Ecology that can unite religion and science, and the love that can unite the warring factions within each. The elites that followed Constantine and Solvay have somehow lost the plot. But the times are changing.

5

Matter, Spirit and Being

Matter (Latin 'materia': wood, timber ... from 'mater' — mother —
denoting the trunk of a tree regarded as the mother of its offshoots)
Latin. spīritus ... breathing, breath, air, etc ... The animating
or vital principle
Be: from Sanskrit bhū-, bhaw-, Greek phy- ... The primary sense
appears to have been 'to occupy a place'

The split between rational and intuitive, or between religion and science, is often described in terms of "matter and spirit". Matter, in the days before quantum theory, was thought to be mechanical, definite and (according to scientists) real. Spirit, on the other hand, was subtle, intuitive, ungraspable and (according to non-scientists) even more real. This view went together with the traditional picture of the universe, derived from Greek thinking, as a series of concentric spheres with the earth at the centre and heaven at the outermost limit, beyond the stars. Despite space-travel and the Hubble telescope, this view continues today. I recall once attending a funeral service where the priest, extemporising in the sermon, suggested that the Dear Departed was, even at this moment, passing through the outer stars of the galaxy! In the early Christian period, it was thought that matter got steadily more light and fluffy as one went outwards, or upwards as seen from the earth, starting with the sticky goo of the earth we tread on, turning into the shining material of the stars, and finishing up with "spirit", totally weightless, inviscid, transparent etc. This picture led to a very up-and-down theology. Up was good, down was bad, and we're more or less at the bottom. In the words of the creed debated at the Council of Nicaea, Jesus "came down from heaven" and subsequently "ascended into heaven". Humanity was stuck at the bottom, and needed to be thrown a life-line in order to be hauled up to a more respectable place.

As the reader will have noted, I take none of these ideas seriously, so I was surprised when on one occasion (in the event evoked at the start of this book) I found myself suddenly impressed by words that seemed to affirm an "up and down" universe. I had just got to the end of writing, over a period of more than a year, a long and detailed paper on the foundations of quantum theory. As I was scrolling through the final version, the verbalised thought *"the descent of Spirit into the arms of Matter"* was suddenly in my mind, accompanied by that turbulent emotion that comes when one sees or hears something almost unbearably beautiful, bringing tears to the eyes — that nameless emotion that the poet Rilke evoked, writing: "beauty is just the start of the void, barely endured"[47].

On thinking about what I had been reading recently, and noting the words "into the arms", I realised, however, that what I was recalling was not the vertical cosmology of fourth century Christianity, but William Blake's spiritual and political epic *The Marriage of Heaven and Hell*. What Blake was mythically envisaging was not the rescuing of humanity from "Hell", but the uniting of the energy of our earthly state with the brilliance of our intellectual state, each of which was pining away because of their separation. To change the mythology, he was looking for the salvation carried by Artemis in Chapter 2, who brought these two realms together in her life. William Blake, who was a poet, an artist and an engraver, produced the editions of this book himself by first printing the pages and then ornamenting them by hand with both large pictures and minute decorations intertwining with the lines of text. On many pages there appears, in between the lines of text, one or more pictures of two figures, their bodies horizontal, literally flying towards each other with outstretched arms, representing the body and the soul, the two aspects of ourselves that had become separated. This vital dimension was what I had left out of my turgid physics paper.

In this chapter I want to make sense of this idea, and in order to do this I need to develop a concept of matter that is quite different both from the fourth century image of earth as a lump of goo at the centre of the universe, and from the nineteenth century billiard-ball atoms driven by Newton's laws of mechanics. I will be chasing a more elusive concept of matter that is pointed to, but not explained, both by quantum theory and by religion: matter as the source of being; matter that is not in opposition to spirit, but one side of a coin whose other side is spirit.

*   *   *   * *** *   *   *

I need to start further back, however. Matter is what things are made of, and so we must first talk about *making*.

Civilised people (people who live in a *civis*, Latin for city) make things; as opposed to heathens (people who live on the heath) who live in caves and throw stones at passing rabbits. Civilised people drive off to their nearest DIY store, buy the timber and screws and wall plugs, take it home and set to putting up a shelf. Or, at a more basic level, they might hew down a tree, strip the branches from a tree, put the trunk (the *mater* or "mother" of the branches) over a saw-pit, and get to work cutting the planks. One way or the other, if you are civilised and want to make something you get hold of the *mater*ials.

There is a lovely thirteenth century book illustration in the National Library in Vienna of "God creating the world". He appears as a rather shrewd looking man in church robes holding a pair of dividers (for measuring and constructing precise angles) bending over a shapeless lump as he gets ready to start making a cosmos out of it. The artist for the book obviously couldn't get his head round the theological doctrine that God made the universe out of nothing. Surely even God had to have materials?

Officially, God was supposed to have been like Alderman Sir Sidney Kimber J.P. who, according to a plaque in my home city, "conceived and brought into being" Southampton sports centre, perhaps without ever touching a shovel in his life. But God and Sidney Kimber presumably had a team of stout angels/workmen who got their hands dirty with whatever matter was needed to make a cosmos/sports centre with. So where did that matter come from?

In our science today we face the same sort of problem as did the artist who drew "God creating the world". We need to track down matter. What is the cosmos made of? Atoms. What are atoms made of? Protons and electrons. And then it's quarks and gluons, and then the inflaton field, and then the false vacuum... the list looks as though it could go on forever. As every child being put to bed knows, the best way to stay up late is to follow up a simple question with a "why?" to each attempted answer your doting father gives to you; or in this case keep asking, "and what's that made of?" There seems to be no getting away from the fact that if you make something you need some matter; but equally, the concept seems to lead to what philosophers call an "infinite regress" (what the child calls "never going to bed"). You can attempt to get to bed-time by answering "it's made out of nothing", but that leads straight to Leibniz's ultimate question, "so why is there something rather than nothing?" Checkmate.

One attractive way out of this conundrum, for those from the Judaic/Christian/Islamic tradition, is to bring God into it, and then use a bit of fancy footwork to evade the infinite regress. God *is* existence and God's existence is in eternity, outside of time, in a single infinitely capacious Now. So there is no "before" to worry about, and God's existence derives from God's own self, so there is no need for anything beyond God. According to this approach, in this infinite Now, God "conceives and brings into being" matter itself, and time along with it. From there on, science can take over.

There are strong parallels between this and the debates about the Trinity discussed in the last chapter. Just as the Father *begets* the Son, so the Father and the Son *create* (bring into being) the universe. (The Holy Spirit can be thrown in for good measure, though this is not really necessary at this point.) There is, however, a careful distinction between the begetting of the Son and the creation of matter, to do with what these things are made of. The Son is "of one substance" with the Father, so that they are equivalent and have the same status. The universe, on the other hand, is made of matter, which is created by God and is subordinate to God.

So both religion and the science of Newton were tying themselves into hopeless knots in their attempts to produce a rational account of our intuitive awareness of pure vibrant *being*. We encounter once again the fundamental division of knowing into two distinct parts, the rational and the intuitive, and if we ignore this division the answers we come up with tend to be fanciful nonsense that satisfies neither reason nor intuition. In this chapter I want to explore the history of the idea of matter in order to understand the problem of matter better. We can then turn to quantum theory, when we will see the idea of matter dissolve before our eyes into a different language of paradox, which offers hope for finding a solution.

*   *   * * **** *   *   *

The single most important idea in the history of matter, an idea that remains as vital today as it was in ancient Greece, was formulated by the philosopher Plato. His shadow, and his light, hangs over the past 2400 years of Western thought. He transmitted through his works the spirit of his teacher and spiritual master Socrates[48]; he founded the Academy in Athens which nurtured philosophical inquiry in Greece for 300 years; and from his teaching grew the quasi-religious movement of Neo-Platonism which contributed to both Christianity and Sufism. An additional strand of the history was the approach of Aristotle, Plato's student. He started a line of thinking which stood in opposition to Platonism though it still operated within the concepts and methods that Plato had laid down. Aristotle's thought came to dominate Western Europe from the 13th century on.

Plato's work is known to us through a series of about 30 books, most of which present his ideas in the form of an imaginary dialogue between a philosopher (usually Plato's own charismatic teacher Socrates) and a group of students, often augmented by a visiting guest philosopher or eminent person. The books are usually referred to by the name of the featured visitor. Most of them were preserved by Christian and Islamic scholars in Eastern Europe and Spain, but only gradually found their way into Western Europe during the Middle Ages[49]. The most important of these for ideas about matter is the dialogue *Timaeus*, which was also one of the most widely known. Here Plato describes the fundamental principles on which the universe is based, which includes an account of the "four elements", the most well known early concept of matter (first formulated by Empedocles a century before Plato). In addition, however, it contains a deeper theory of matter that is more interesting, and much more relevant to modern physics.

There are three basic notions in this system. First comes the realm of what Plato calls the *eidōn*, translated as "ideas" or "forms": eternal blueprints that govern all existence[50]. The corresponding thing for us would perhaps be the laws of physics —

though these lack the specific detail of Plato's forms. Plato describes the realm of *eidōn* in the Timaeus as follows:

"Wherefore also we must acknowledge that there is one kind of being which is always the same, uncreated and indestructible, never receiving anything into itself from without, nor itself going out to any other, but invisible and imperceptible by any sense, and of which the contemplation is granted to intelligence only."

Then there are the actual things that we observe around us with our senses. These depend on the *eidōn* that govern their coming into being, without which they cannot exist:

"And there is another nature of the same name with it [the *eidōn*], and like to it, perceived by sense, created, always in motion, becoming in place and again vanishing out of place, which is apprehended by opinion and sense."

And finally, introduced by Plato almost apologetically, there is *chora*, which means "place" or "space":

"And there is a third nature, which is space, and is eternal, and admits not of destruction and provides a home for all created things, and is apprehended without the help of sense, by a kind of spurious reason, and is hardly real; which we beholding as in a dream, say of all existence that it must of necessity be in some place and occupy a space, but that what is neither in heaven nor in earth has no existence."[51]

The eternal forms (or "ideas") determine *what* a thing is, whether it is a bed, or a horse etc. But knowing a form, whether of a horse or a unicorn, does not conjure up the thing itself, or specify the particular individual instance of the form that we are talking about. Forms are general, things are particular, so that we can distinguish (by pointing) "this horse here" from "that horse there". Things have "thisness" as well as form, and thisness, says Plato, derives from space. He also implies, by his description of *chora,* that existence as well as thisness also derives from space.

The physicist John Wheeler often used to tell a story at physics seminars to illustrate this whole problem of the relation between form and existence. In this modern case, in place of "forms" we have physical "laws".

"Imagine," he would say, "a physicist who is in quest of the ultimate secret of the universe." We would listen attentively, because that was our quest also.

"She has finally found the secret of unifying all the fundamental forces of the universe, and has written out the governing equations of the universe on several large sheets of paper. She spreads them out in front of her" (here Wheeler used eloquent mime and gestures) "and proclaims, 'here is the source of the universe: now a new universe can come into being.'

"But nothing happens."

Laws or forms can specify *how* or *what* things are, but existence, being, thisness, *that* things are ... seems wrapped in mystery. So Plato introduces *chora,* which elsewhere he describes as "the nurse of becoming", to provide the possibility of a "here" or a "this" and so to call into being actual images of the eternal forms.

Plato's *chora* is an attempted ultimate stopping point for the question, "what is matter?" He achieves this by recognising that there is something more fundamental than "what is it made of?", a something to do with being and thisness. This is what the quest for matter is really about; get hold of this and it will provide a stopping point for the question, "but what is *that* made of?" For something to exist, says Plato, it has to exist somewhere ("in heaven or on earth"). So the "somewhere", *chora,* is the ultimate origin of being. "Somewhere" does not need a further "somewhere" for it to find a place, because it already is itself a place. Matter, in this ultimate sense, beyond the idea of making, is what enables actual existence.

The same issue comes up in physics. Wheeler raised the question, but could not answer it. For Einstein what enabled existence, the ultimate foundation, was space-time, a modern variation on Plato's *chora* or space. But in modern physics space-time itself is subject to "what is *that* made of?" We will see later that this question converges on the ultimate questions about religion and humanity, as all three questions converge on the area of new forms of logic, the area of the intuitive.

I want to stress a paradoxical difficulty emerging here with the picture of a universe with spirit or form at the top and matter or *chora* at the bottom. The problem is that, as Plato himself emphasises, *both of these* seem essential for that other great philosophical concept, "being" or "existence". Perhaps we need to stop thinking in terms of a linear up-and-down universe, and instead bend the chain of being into a circle, in which matter and spirit are combined in a single source of being. We will return to this later, looking at the image of the ouroboros, the snake that eats its tail.

* * * * *** * * * *

The relationship between form and matter (or being) is important in all this, but it is sometimes hard to grasp. The problem is that matter, the stuff that supports the form of an object, is defined negatively. It is whatever is not form. So the idea of matter, or being, is paradoxical because its importance lies in what it is not. I have found, however, that this notion becomes real and tangible in the context of the natural world — the world which, I am claiming, holds the key to uniting Eros and Psyche, religion and science.

So I invite you to join me in imagination when I was sitting at the edge of a stretch of woodland, where it dissolved and merged into grassland; sitting on the uncertain boundary where the light of the sun was fractured by overhanging branches. As I sat, I became aware of the abundance of different forms. My gaze enlarged another five centimetres, and another, and another, and each time I became aware of more different species of plants and animals that were with me in this place — different varieties of grass, different flowers, a different insect or spider. And surely I was seeing and recognising only a tiny fraction of what was there in totality. In addition, each individual was unique in its species, each blade of grass different, each leaf — carrying its own little colony of inhabitants — a different metropolis. Multitude upon multitude of different forms were in front of me, filling me with amazement and exhilaration.

This is the delight of *form*, which rejoices in diversity. Form, in fact, *is* diversity: a thing has form because one part is different from another part, because they are in different places or have different qualities. Nature loves diversification, an essential aspect of form.

So to discover matter we have to look at the opposite of form, the opposite of diversity. As a first step in the quest for matter, let us switch our imagination to recall looking at one single thing. In order to focus completely on its uniqueness and individuality, I will go the whole way and imagine the person I most love. When we are with such a person, we recognise not their form, but their essence, the "who" that they are underneath the form. It could be argued that we recognise them *through* their form, but we still have a clear sense of their being who they are. *Being* strikes you like a revelation, accompanied by our old friend "the numinous", or "the sacred". We recognise that *being* comes to us through our intuition while form involves also our rational, "thinking" side; but we are encountering one single universe before us.

When we look at the Christian mystic Eckhart, we will again encounter this idea of being as "what is not" (i.e. "not form"), something negative but at the same time supremely real and present.

* * * * *** * * *

Plato's pupil Aristotle was a more down to earth thinker, who had no truck with the idea of a realm of eternal forms. He still held "form" to be an essential component of each thing, but argued that the form of a thing was not derived from an eternal instruction manual, but was simply an essential part of the thing itself. Like Plato, he needed another ingredient to specify the thisness of a thing, and he called this ingredient *hyle*, which means "timber" or, as we would say, matter.

This was more or less how the situation was left until the seventeenth century, the time of the two creators of the modern era, Descartes and Newton. Descartes' answer to the problem of existence was to introduce two different types of matter. The first was *res extensa* (literally "extended stuff"). This was a type of basic existence whose defining property was spatial extension – which was almost exactly the same idea as Plato's *chora*. The only difference was that, while *chora* was vague and indistinct, relying on forms to give it any sort of definite quantities or qualities, *res extensa* came in discrete blobs (or "corpuscles"), which stacked together to produce as much space as called for by the circumstances.

Descartes' other type of matter was *res cogitans* or "thinking stuff", which produced souls. This had nothing to do with space, and was intellectual in nature. Souls were, however, associated with bodies, and hence space, in a way that he never really satisfactorily explained[52]. Although he never dabbled with this area himself[53], Descartes was now coming very close to the ideas of "substance" and "hypostasis" that had rocked the church 1300 years earlier.

Newton's contribution was to separate the discreteness of Descartes' corpuscles from the idea of space. His matter drew on the old idea of *atoms*: distinct particles that could not be divided, and his atoms, unlike Descartes' "corpuscles" were *in* space, an infinite absolute space, rather than *making* space. So Plato's *chora* had split into two components: particles and space. And the word "matter", corresponding to Aristotle's *hyle,* was applied only to particles.

For Newton, actual physical existence was existence of matter (atoms) in space. There was also spiritual existence, of God and souls, but this was a quite separate category, like Descartes' *res cogitans.* As far as physics was concerned, without particles in space there could be no actual things.

This is the picture that gave the delegates at the Solvay conference so much trouble. By that time, with the first steps in quantum theory, atoms had turned from indivisible nuggets to orbiting particles, and then the particles had disappeared into mathematics and paradox. Space-time hung on, but in the twentieth century it was realised that this too had to be brought under the dissolving enchantment of quantum theory. By the time quantum theory was fully developed, 2400 years of human thinking about matter had come to an end. The Solvay conference was the beginning of the end: quantum theory was about to redefine the nature of existence.

Apart from John Wheeler, physicists are rarely concerned with philosophical questions about "existence". And yet this concern is being forced upon them. Once it was the case that what existed was matter, and there was no problem with either "existence" or "matter". But then with quantum theory it became more and more uncertain what matter was, and more and more uncertain what actually existed and what was just a sort of fuzzy possibility.

From the start of quantum theory onwards, physics has investigated what happens at progressively smaller length

scales. Atoms, once the constituents of matter on which everything larger depended, were broken down into smaller parts, and
these were further broken down by using higher and higher
energies in large particle accelerators, leading up to the "super
hadron collider" at the European research institute CERN. Each
soaks up more money and energy, and confers more prestige on
its builders, than the last. Atoms are now seen as large cumbrous
structures with many more layers beneath them. And so, the
basis for physics, the starting point of particles that were "fundamental", has kept shifting to smaller length scales, and so shifting
to theories that are progressively more speculative and harder to
test. The notion of "matter" has receded into an obscurity of
increasing theoretical complexity, where only optimists expect a
final resolution.

I will return to quantum theory to continue this story in a later
chapter. But matter will not be explained by quantum theory: we
will need to combine quantum theory with the insights of
religion, and so we will turn to that next to see what religion has
to say about "being".

* * * * * *** * * * *

"Being" is perhaps the single biggest issue within the whole
sweep of philosophy, generating whole libraries full of
discussion and ideas. But within both Western religions and the
Hindu tradition, the mystics — by which I mean, people who
appear to have direct experience of ultimate reality — speak
about "being" unambiguously. They declare that being is
beyond rational thought. Rationality can, by its very nature, only
tell us *how* something is. *That* it is, and what the source of this is,
comes through immediate intuitive experience, before reasoning
starts.

What mystics see and proclaim with complete clarity, we can
catch glimpses of in everyday life, glimpses that enlarge and

heighten our life, that make life supremely worth living. I have already described how being is discerned by contemplating one whom you love. Indeed, the awareness of the presence of pure being is the essence of love, of the Eros from which we started in Chapter 1. Eros arises when you truly see who or what another person or place is: when you stand before this Other and your inner eye opens, to see that what is before you simply *is* — in her/his/its own intrinsic splendour. As I have noted, this experience is also the experience of the sacred, which we earlier identified as the core of religion.

So rather than relying solely on rationality to explore "being", let us look at one of the most profound Western mystical writers, Meister Eckhart. He was born around 1260 in Germany, became a member of the Dominican religious order, trained in theology in Paris, and spent the latter part of his life actively preaching in Germany. At this time the Western church was deeply suspicious of any who deviated from conservative views, and charges of heresy were levelled at Eckhart, which he stoutly repudiated.

His word for being was "isness" (*istikeit*) which he identified as the defining quality of the source of reality (a source which Eckhart, in his Christian tradition, of course calls "God" – though with qualification, as we shall shortly see). We cannot know *about* this quality of isness, in the sense of verbal knowledge, because the verbal and the rational can only grasp *how* and *what* things are, not isness itself. But the mystic can know isness *directly* as she follows the path of becoming one with God, by "sinking into God":

"You should, in the eternal Now, sink and flow away your 'you' into His 'his', and your 'you' should so become one 'my' in His 'my' that you will eternally know with Him His sourceless 'isness' and His nameless nothingness."[54]

Eckhart is saying here that you must get rid of all labels and particular forms of being in order to experience being, "isness", itself. So you must get rid of personal being — "I" or "you" — and get rid of religious labels that say that God (being) is this, that or the other. Getting rid of all labels is the essence of Eckhart's spirituality. When all labels go, then you are left, he says here, with "nothingness". Indeed, there is not even God here because this label has gone. Elsewhere he writes, "I pray God to rid me of God"[55]. On the spectrum from the verbal/rational to the intuitive we are here at the extreme end of the intuitive, when everything verbal has fallen away.

But this "isness", or being, is not something static or passive. On the contrary, it is the source of all being. Isness cannot be separated from creative activity. In response to the question of how isness originates being, the mystic does not, however, answer directly. The mystic knows (but cannot in truth say, because words destroy what is to be said) that "There Is" and that isness overflows into all being. This is what the Council of Nicaea was trying to express in mythological form when it debated the relation between the Father and the Son. The mythical "begetting" which caused them so much trouble at the rational level is, according to Eckhart[56], the overflowing of pure isness into the relationship of Father and Son, and this overflowing continues into the creation of the cosmos. So in the union between God and the mystic, where she knows the nature of God, she knows also her own isness as one with absolute isness. Isness cannot be divided or a distinction made between "mine" and "God's" because isness is above all such forms and structures. This isness is active in creating, it is the verb "be-ing" as much as the noun "being", and that creative capacity is experienced as a part of the mystic him/herself as much as it is a part of God.

"God must simply become me and I must become God — so completely that this "he" and this "I" share one "is" and in this "isness" do one work eternally."[57]

* * * * *** * * * *

This may sound very remote from our own lives, so I will give another example from my own experience of the natural world, a very direct experience that in fact reminded me of Eckhart when I started writing this chapter. It happened in the course of a "co-operative inquiry", which is a widely recognised systematically structured way of comparing and analysing experiences between different people. I and six others had come together to examine the factors that affected our relationships with the world around us. On several successive days between two of our residential sessions I carried out the "homework" for that period in Southampton Common. I was in a part of it that had been cleared a few years previously, allowing an undergrowth of saplings to grow, which by this time had started to shape themselves into distinct clumps of young trees. I sat in front of one of these and, as I sat, I got to know this clump more intimately and began to feel its presence more clearly.

But while my thoughts and emotions were certainly being influenced by this vegetation, and its appearance to me was influenced by my thoughts, this was still a relationship at arm's length. I was sensitive to what the clump meant *to me,* but this was a much shallower feeling than that of a relationship with a person whose inner being I might (so I supposed) touch with empathy. And so I was led to ask the clump the question, what is its inner being, what is its being not for me but *for itself?*

I had in the past asked questions of trees, expecting and receiving an answer, but that had always been within the context of my own world-picture, of the projections that the tree would allow me to place on it. Now I was attempting to put aside these human constructions and to ask, with a feeling of deference, but also of urgency, about the trees' own world.

I immediately realised that this was an impossible question. What language, what emotion, had I in common with this small ecosystem, whereby it could transmit to me anything that I could receive? This recognition of impossibility was itself answer enough for the time being. My question had been generously rewarded by a view of the unscaleable precipice between the trees and I.

On my next visit I repeated the question, holding the intent to explore this precipice in more detail. There was no answer. More exactly, the answer was silence. I began to savour this silence. It was like the silence that surrounds each phrase of a plainsong chant; a silence that flows into the place of the dying echoes, and is articulated by the fading of the surrounding words.

As I again repeated this experience, I discovered that I had been wrong to assume that there was no common ground between my inner being and that of the clump. I perceived that its reply of silence was identical to the silence at the heart of my own being. Because for me, meditation is like plainsong: attenuating the thoughts and words until the silence that surrounds them becomes lucid.

I suggest that this is a pointer to the *nihtheit* (nothingness) that Eckhart had experienced in its totality, as ultimate being.

* * * * *** * * *

So far I have mainly followed the "matter" pole of the spirit-matter polarity. Matter was seen as the "that" which makes being possible, in conjunction with form, and from this point of view matter was defined negatively, as Plato's *chora*, empty in itself and as a result of this allowing being. This led me to Eckhart's nothingness, lying beyond the contradictions of opposites that faced his mystical journey, and beyond the apparent opposition of spirit and matter. Eckhart's is the negative way, involving stripping away form and distinction, in an increasingly both-and logic, in the pursuit of the ultimate.

But there is also the other pole, the route that follows spirit or form, which involves a positive way, seeking the ultimate in terms of clarity and comprehensiveness: the ultimate theory of everything, or in Plato's terminology the "form" of the supreme good[58] that provides a standard against which to judge all value. The Platonic view, handed down into the Christian tradition, is that being requires both positive and negative poles. But as one pursues this ultimate form, so things become not only more luminous, but also more simple. Each successive physical theory, by integrating the essences of the previous separate and more *ad hoc* theories, becomes more simple. Each deeper form of morality subsumes a multitude of previous separate laws and conventions and so becomes simpler. So this way also is a stripping away, a losing; but a losing that is seen as a gain.

In many traditions, these two ways, of stripping away to the darkest matter and of stripping away to the highest form or principle, are seen as coming together in a single ultimate. This is the point of the night from which "comes the fullness of light" described by St John of the Cross[59] or the "inchoate" of Frederick Parker-Rhodes which we shall meet in a later chapter. The process of joining the extremes is often depicted as the ouroboros, (Greek for tail-eater) as in the striking diagram below introduced by Joel Primack[60], and after him Bernard Carr. Around the ouroboros, from tail to head, are depicted objects of a steadily increasing size, covering the whole length scale of existence, from the smallest at which it makes sense to talk about space at all, to the length scale of the entire physical cosmos. The scale is marked out in steps, each one being 100000 times the size of the previous one. It is remarkable that living organisms such as we know on earth, including, incidentally, ourselves, occupy the exact middle of this scale, opposite to the point of total unity. This is no coincidence: this scale of size is large enough to carry a rich complexity of organisation, but small enough to operate as a single coherent system. Make it 100 larger, or 100 times smaller, and one or other of these properties of a living organism will fail.

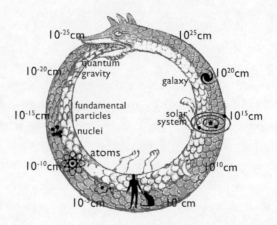

The cosmic ouroborus, based on a concept by Joel Primack. The length scales, labelled in centimetres and equally positioned round the ouroboros, increase from tail to head so that each is 100000 times the size of the previous one.

So as we move in our mind from this central position, we move away from the living and into the progressively more Other. Until we finally reach, in one direction, the entire cosmos, and in the other direction, the most fundamental level of matter. The ancient alchemical symbol of the ouroboros shows these two extremes united in the mouth grasping the tail. Physically this represents the origin of the universe, its earliest phase, for which there was no "before", when the entire universe was contained in a size of the most fundamental elements of matter. In terms of being, as we have seen, this is the point where pure being is emptied of all its qualities, so far from our rational concepts as to be beyond words, accessible only by mystical intuition. This being overflows into all existence, at all scales.

One vital understanding in all this is the way in which there is no sudden leap from the rational and scientific into the non-rational and mystical. Rather, these two ways of knowing are complementary to each other at each length scale, each requiring the other in order to make sense. But as we pass, in either direction, towards the serpent's head and tail, so the verbal recedes in significance. It is replaced, not only by the intuitive which we have discussed, but also by the mathematical (akin to the ideas of Plato). It is as if the mathematical, being detached and abstracted from concrete words while remaining totally rational, is in a position to mediate between the conceptual and the intuitive.

I have talked so far from the human perspective of going out in two directions in order to find our deeper origins. But if we start from the other end — from our origins and the origins of the universe — then we begin at the inchoate point, the tail-mouth. From this comes the earliest expression in the primordial universe of a distinction between space-time and law, a simple polarity (called by Plato the "indefinite dyad"). From this then emerges the driving dynamic of the universe, the process of spirit calling being out of matter. Until at the opposite point of the Ouroboros, we find spirit re-entering the arms of matter.

6

Truth

True: from Old English tréowe, 'having good faith'. Hence honest ...
sincere ... genuine.

In the preceding chapters I have shed doubt on many attempts in the past to fit the universe into a tidy logical framework. But this only sharpens and makes more urgent the fundamental questions: What is the world really like? How can we human beings *know*? Are we to trust rationality or intuition? All these circle around the notion of truth. Whatever answer we give to these questions, we will ask, "but is that really true?" In this chapter I will describe the way in which truth is bound up with ideas about logic, and the way that logic emerged historically, and subsequently evolved. This will lead on to a discussion of quantum theory in the following chapter, when we move towards a solution of these puzzles.

In a famous passage from the Gospel of John in the Bible, Jesus tells Pilate "For this I have come into the world, to bear witness to the truth. Every one who is of the truth hears my voice." And Pilate said to him, "What is truth?", but did not stay to hear an answer[61].

This discourse makes more sense in the original Greek than it does in English, for the Greek for 'truth', *alētheia*, literally means "uncoveredness", implying direct vision, or disclosure. So the conversation is about achieving inner vision, or experiencing a revelation of understanding. This is the sort of truth that is involved in religion, as I described it in Chapter 3: a truth not about statements of fact, but about adopting a "way", an orientation of the mind based on a particular insight into the way the world is. This has resonances with the original meanings of the English word 'truth', which are to do with trustworthiness, authenticity and the like. We are turned to follow a way because of a disclosure that strikes us as worthy of trust. So originally "truth" implied something personal, a matter of judgement and trust based on a disclosure.

Importantly, this sort of truth is not an either/or matter. It will tend to be a matter of degree, since people can be more or less trustworthy and disclosures can be more or less clear. The dominant modern scientific concept of truth tends, however, to be completely different from this. Truth here is about *statements* (also called *propositions*) irrespective of who makes them, and a statement is regarded as true if it is a fact, corresponding to the actual state of affairs. Statements, if understood in this way, are either true or false.

I will try to chart the very devious progression from the original concept to this modern one. Once we stand back and look at this history, we will see that it points to a concept of truth that is rather different from the dominant modern one, and which makes better sense of both science and religion. The philosophy of 'truth' is vast and complicated[62]. It raises questions about the nature of the world (are "facts" really "out there"?) about the nature of knowledge and about the nature of language. This chapter tries to touch the edge of some of these issues.

* * * * *** * * * *

The older concept of truth did not necessarily have anything do with language at all. The "flower sermon" attributed (contrary to the evidence) to the Buddha consisted, it is said, of his holding up a single flower in silence. Given the overall context, those present experienced *alētheia*, a disclosure, with no words spoken.

But it is much more common for truth to be linked with language, and at the time of the Buddha a profound change was already taking place in the way people used language and the relation of language to truth. Logic, a new way of using language, was starting to appear.

According to Karen Armstrong[63], this change towards logic had started in Western Europe around 650 BCE as a result of changes in society, and particularly changes in the nature of warfare. At this period of Greek history warfare stopped being solely an activity of aristocrats, and became instead the duty of an army made up of all citizens, who fought side by side to defend each Greek city-state against aggression by the others. This led to the democratisation of society: "A farmer who fought next to a noblemen in the phalanx would never see the aristocracy in the same way again. It would not be long before the lower classes demanded that that *their* organization – the people's assembly – should take a central role in the government of the city." But this was not just a change in politics, but also a change in the way people spoke and thought. Previously all public speaking had been in the language of the aristocratic hero, the language of the epic stories and myths of Homer. The new army, however, was concerned not with myths but with *logos* (dialogue-speech). "On the battlefields and in councils of war", writes Armstrong, "soldiers confronted questions of life and death. Instead of asking, 'What is the ultimate meaning of this event?' the men of *logos* asked, 'What happened?' and 'What shall we do?'" [64]

Whether or not the military influence described by Armstrong was really its main cause, the style of Greek public speech progressively changed from the mythic to something more factual, until a century or more later a fully fledged logical approach was being taught by the founder of Greek philosophy, Socrates. All we know about him comes from the accounts of his work written by his pupil, Plato, as I described in the last chapter.

Although the actual content of these works is probably largely fictional, there is no reason to doubt that Socrates' general approach and method was correctly described.

This method was the philosophical dialogue. A group of people come together and carefully and attentively discuss the meaning of a basic concept like "Love" or "Justice". Socrates is depicted as taking a very dominant role in this, asking of the others a succession of leading questions designed to draw out and scrutinise the ideas. Logic is here not been used as a method for generating the truth directly; rather, it is being used as a tool to disclose whether or not the participants' ideas are sound. And the answer reached in the dialogues run by Socrates is almost invariably, no, the ideas being advanced by the other party are contrary to logic and so basically unsound. So the participants are thrown back on examining the deeper source within themselves of their ideas and the actions that follow from them. For Socrates truth still lay in understanding oneself and knowing ones inner motivations; but truth was now assumed to be logical, so that if one's ideas were found contrary to logic, then truth demanded their amendment.

The role of logic, therefore, was to keep open this intuitive inner knowledge. Logic was not contrary to intuition, but was a means of allowing it to be expressed clearly and reliably. Instead of blindly responding to one's intuitions, Socrates and his immediate forerunners identified a clear logical method which deepened intuition (inner knowledge) and made it more trustworthy; that is, more truthful.

But logic, while it could help reach the truth, was no cast iron guarantee of truth: it depended on how the speaker used logic. A skilful manipulator of words, whether a newspaper editor or a politician on television, can persuade us to believe what he wants us to believe, and he can bring in logic to make his argument appear solid. There is a big difference between the *dialogue* of Socrates, which is used to uncover the truth and the *rhetoric* of most public speakers who, in Socrates' time as in our own, used words and logic to bend ideas towards the speaker's desire. While the Councils of Nicaea and Solvay, examined earlier, might have been conceived in terms of the discovery of truth, what actually happened (certainly at Nicaea) had as much, or more, to do with rhetoric than with dialogue.

To give an idea of what logic is all about, I will describe the approach of Aristotle, Plato's pupil and the first person to attempt to make logic systematic. On his view, a logical discussion started with statements, called *premises*, which everyone agreed on, then these could be pieced together to form new statements. The trick was to specify the right way of doing the piecing together so that the resulting new statement would always be true, provided that the agreed initial premises were true. Logic, therefore, depended on a set of correct rules for piecing together statements.

The set of rules proposed by Aristotle involved connecting pairs of statements, each of a particular sort. The standard example involves combining the statement

"All men are mortal"

with the statement

"Socrates is a man"

to deduce the statement

"Socrates is mortal".

This is a set of three statements, two given and one deduced, involving three elements ("man", "mortal", "'Socrates"), with one of the elements (man) in both of the given statements but not in the deduced statement. A scheme like this is called a *syllogism*.

There are lots of different sorts of syllogisms, corresponding to variations on the form of the statements by introducing qualifiers such as "some" or "not" so as to produce structures like "some heroes are not mortal", "no dogs are heroes" etc. Aristotle proposed that every argument could be broken down into a series of syllogisms, and he then classified all syllogisms into those that were *valid,* leading from true premises to true conclusions, and those which were *invalid,* liable to lead to false conclusions.

The key insight of Aristotle was to see that truth and validity were different things. Consider, for example, the syllogism

"Some heroes are not mortal,
no dogs are heroes;
hence all dogs are mortal."

This is an invalid syllogism, even though in this case it happens to lead from (possibly) true premises to a true conclusion. It has the same structure as the syllogism

"Some fruits are not apples,
no potatoes are fruits;
hence all potatoes are apples."

which leads from true premises to a false conclusion, something that is always a danger with an invalid syllogism. So an invalid syllogism cannot be part of a reliable argument.

A logical argument had to be valid, expressible as a series of valid syllogisms; if that were the case then the result, Aristotle claimed, would definitely be true if the premises were true. An illogical argument, on the other hand, (as often used in rhetoric) might happen to come up with the truth, but there was no guarantee of this.

Although I am a mathematician by training, I find ploughing

through Aristotelian syllogisms like this a depressing experience (and Aristotle has produced two books full of this sort of stuff). It is depressing because almost no one actually reasons like this. Reasoning with syllogisms (or with their equivalents in modern logic) is like drinking soup with a paintbrush: you know you'll get there in the end but it's so ponderous and unpleasant that you don't even want to start. In practice we don't reason logically, we speed things up with a good mixture of intuition and rules-of-thumb. It's not strictly logical, but it's quick and works well most of the time. When it comes to deciding what to do in conversation with others, we need the skill of judging how much to take for granted, when to use short cuts in the reasoning, and when to move more towards logic. All this we do intuitively. And when the discussion starts using more logical forms, we need intuition to warn us when speakers are twisting the argument to serve their own ends, so that their speech becomes rhetoric, rather than logic. The skill of living in society involves honing one's intuition to achieve all this.

To explore this more closely, it is worth comparing Aristotle's and Socrates' approaches to "dialogue". A good illustration of the difference between the two concerns the notion of a "theorem" – a demonstration of a mathematical truth. In the book by Plato which depicts an imaginary dialogue between Socrates and the philosopher Meno (so the book is known simply as *Meno*), Socrates wishes to show that we have access to innate knowledge about eternal truths, of which mathematical truths are a part. He therefore asks Meno to call one of his slaves, presumably someone with no familiarity with mathematics or intellectual debate, and Socrates then conducts the slave through what we would call the "proof" of a simple geometrical theorem. The process, however, is not one of formal logic, but one of drawing a series of diagrams so that the slave could *see* a succession of geometric relationships, leading to seeing the truth of the final proposition. Indeed the word "theorem" comes from *theoria*, meaning "seeing", and the proof of the theorem here is not so much a logical argument as an opening of an inner eye with which to see the truth. This is very similar to the whole process of dialogue as it is understood by Plato, and to some extent, probably, by Socrates. Plato's seeing — or, as he usually calls it, "recalling" – corresponds to the rather loose term "intuition" that I have been using here.

The notion of "theorem" is quite different today, however. It is essentially an Aristotelian notion: a theorem is a sequence of formulae, each one of which follows by strict logic from the preceding ones, starting with the basic premises of the mathematical system that is being used.

Aristotle and Plato had basically different understandings of logic and truth. Aristotle's truth (in the spirit of the talk of military men which Armstrong emphasised) was a collection of concrete, no-nonsense facts, like "either the sickle is in the shed or it is in the garden." For things like this the rigid structure of syllogisms, though ponderous, does work. Aristotle hoped that this approach could be extended from the mundane to the whole structure of the cosmos.

Plato started not from the world of sickles and sheds but from a profound belief in the existence of the "ideas", the world of eternal truths, including the truths of mathematics and capital letter concepts like Justice, Love and Beauty. Though we can to some extent still move around this world by using logic, for Plato it is impossible to dispense with intuiting/seeing. Both Aristotle and Plato agreed, however, that in seeking for the truth they were seeking something absolute, something completely reliable and set apart from the mere "opinion" of those who were not philosophers.

This disparaged "opinion", the view of one particular person or one political faction about what is the case, is not absolute but relative; that is, relative to the person or faction concerned. Putting this another way, it depends on the *context* of what is being discussed. When I remark to my wife that "the geranium leaves are rather yellow" the context is that we are both sitting in the kitchen looking across to the window sill. This context fixes which geraniums I am talking about. Most statements in ordinary conversation need some sort of context if they are to make sense and not be ambiguous. Most significantly, however, my individual, personal context is relevant. The angle from which I am looking, with the sun behind the leaves, may make their appearance quite different from what my wife sees from a different vantage point. If my companion in the kitchen had happened to be blind, then the difference in context would have been even more radical. For my blind companion the geranium leaves perhaps would not have a colour at all as far as she was concerned. She would know that "geranium leaves are green", but for her this might mean that *from a context other than her own* there is a property called colour which has a value called green.

Though practically all my views in everyday conversation are relative, governed by context, I tend to consider that my views are The Truth. It is more comforting to believe that they have the solid foundation of eternal truth; or at least that they are shared by all right-thinking people. So when I meet someone within a different context, I often start off indignantly protesting that they are wrong and I am right. On a larger scale, we might start a fight or a war over it. The charmingly optimistic philosopher Leibniz (whom we met in the last chapter) thought that all human conflict could be avoided provided that everyone reasoned correctly, and he tried to achieve this by using mathematics to do logic. He wrote:

"I am therefore working towards the production of a method which will always be able, for every argument, to cast people's thinking into the form of calculations, so that there will be no need, as now, to raise a fuss, but one could say to another, 'let us calculate'."[65]

At the end of the nineteenth century the analysis of logic had indeed reached the form of turning it into calculations — but there is much more than this to ending conflict! Differences in context mean that, in the human realm, there is no absolute truth.

In the scientific realm, however, it was long hoped that things would be different. Here, surely, is to be found that absolute truth that is so sadly lacking in the human realm, truth independent of any particular context. Galileo, the founder of the science of mechanics in the early seventeenth century, argued that there were certain "primary qualities" such as shape and motion which were absolute and could form the basis of scientific truth, as contrasted with the "secondary qualities" like colour and taste of the human realm which were relative to particular human points of view[66]. The science of physiology would then be able to derive these secondary human perceptions from the primary physical ones. Primary qualities would be "objective", absolutely true, while secondary qualities would be "subjective" and context-dependent.

Logic was essentially bound up with this notion of objectivity. The Platonic emphasis on "seeing" a truth was, for most people in the scientific era, definitely suspect, and anything like intuition was ruled out altogether. The success of science suggested that only objective truth was useful, and only Aristotelian logic could attain to this. But since pure logic is so difficult to apply, relying solely on logic actually makes us more vulnerable to rhetorical manipulation, rather than more secure. For a combination of security and flexibility we need to reach a better balance between logic and seeing, rationality and intuition. This is difficult for Western society, however, because our whole history has been linked to the progressive dominance of Aristotelian logic as the only guide to truth. From the twentieth century on, however, a range of alternative logics started to emerge. In the next section I shall describe the logic that seems to reflect the workings of our intuition, and in the next chapter I shall describe the way that science, and particularly quantum theory, started to promote alternative forms of logic, including more than one system of a type that I will rather loosely call "quantum logic".

*   *   *   * *** *   *   *   *

Our understanding of intuition was radically altered by the work of Sigmund Freud and his introduction of the idea of the "unconscious". Prior to that intuition has either been dismissed as nonsense, or seen as something very mysterious and magical. When Freud suggested that there was a vast area of mental processes of which we were unaware, the area of the unconscious, a new range of possibilities opened up, within which intuition could find a place. I would like now to examine an alternative logic developed by the Chilean psychologist Ignacio Matte Blanco in order to describe how the unconscious behaved[67], which can shed a lot of light on the process of intuitive knowing.

In Freud's practice of psychoanalysis and in our dreams the contents of the unconscious can express itself indirectly through images and quirks of thought that would otherwise be inexplicable. Matte Blanco's starting point was the observation that these expressions of the unconscious did not conform to ordinary logic. We can see this ourselves when we recall our dreams: images are put together in strange ways that have no relation to the logic of ordinary life. A basic tenet of psychoanalysis is that, though the images lack ordinary logic, they have a structure of their own which can be traced through *association*. When the individual is asked to freely associate one word with another, an internal structure is revealed that sheds light on the hidden connections between the images arising from the unconscious.

Matte Blanco pointed out that, in dreams and in the free association of psychoanalysis, concepts or images were associated together, along with a connecting relationship that linked them. So if I were to dream of a particular friend and her daughter these individuals are linked by the relation of daughterhood (and motherhood). Or if I were to dream of a man and a dog, the relationship might be subservience; or if it were a guide-dog it might be support/guidance; or it might be companionship. The point of interest here is that some of these relations are *symmetrical* in that they go both ways: if John is a companion of Roger, it normally follows that Roger is a companion of John. Others are non-symmetrical: if John is feeding Rover then this does not imply that Rover is feeding John. In the course of carrying out much psychoanalysis, Matte Blanco was led to the hypothesis that, in expressing itself through conscious symbols, *the unconscious behaves as if all relations were symmetrical.*

To give a personal example, some time ago I had a vivid dream just before starting on a short course of psychological therapy with a woman therapist (whom I had not yet met), in order to understand myself better. In my dream I was sitting behind a woman friend, supporting her while she gave birth. Dreams are many-faceted, and this one entwined many images; but after careful examination it seemed that the dominating relationship was support (in producing something new) and the dominant characters represented in the dream were myself and the therapist. But the relationship was the wrong way round from the point of view of conventional logic, in that in the therapy the therapist would be supporting me, whereas in the dream "I" was supporting the "therapist" (a role being played by my friend in the dream). The dream was ignoring the normal logical non-symmetry of the relationship of supporting, and treating it as if it were immaterial who was supporting whom. By ignoring the non-symmetry of relationships, the dream was able to bring together ideas more vividly. At face value, I was supporting the "therapist" (the role being played by my friend at this level); but if all relationships are treated as symmetrical, that was the same as the therapist supporting me; and from that point of view I was the one "giving birth" to the new possibilities that

I was anticipating.

So the dream was, like all dreams, manifesting a very strange logic. We can see this logic at play also in our waking thoughts. Though we may try in most of our life to stick to conventional logic, much of our thinking works through associations of ideas, and the unconscious is always insinuating its symbols. In times of stress and of psychological disturbance we are particularly open to this other logic. So in practice we find ourselves operating with a mixture, in variable proportions, of "normal" logic (called by Matte Blanco "asymmetric logic") and the logic that the unconscious produces ("symmetric logic"). Matte Blanco calls this hybrid, by which we actually live, "bilogic".

Bilogic is a contradictory logic, in which all categories start to merge into each other:

> The part is the same as the whole, since if A is a part of B, then by symmetry B is a part of A; but if each is a part of the other then they are the same.

> Extremes on a scale are the same, since if X is the largest in the scale, then X is greater than everything else, so by symmetry everything else is greater than X, so X is least on the scale. Similarly the past is the same as the future, so time does not exist.

If one lets rip with bilogic, the results are wild, mad and mystical, as in this poem by Dunstan Clarke:

> *Dragons are dangerous things*
> *Cats are soft things*
> *Happiness is a contagious thing*
> *London is a derelict roller-coaster*
> *Love is a warm blanket*
> *The hungry want food and*
> *Lovers need their silence*

Dangerous things are dragons
Soft things are cats
Contagious things are happy
Derelict roller-coasters are London
Warm blankets are love
The food wants the hungry and
Silence needs our lovers

My teachers are my students are my parents are our leaders are
     our children not yet born
Are the lights in the sky
As the day is the night so
The heat is the cold so
The rat is the trap
And the trap is the rat

The boundaries are melting away
The living all sleep in their graves
And the dead are walking the streets
The mind is a spider's web
A spider's web is the mind

The healing hands of Hasan-i-Sabah
Have withdrawn themselves from my head
A cocoon of warm unknowing has settled once again
I wrote a symmetrical poem
To awaken the dragons again
Dragons are magical things
Magical things are dragons

*   *   *   * *** *   *   *   *

Matte Blanco's bilogic is an inconsistent logic, in the sense that it leads to statements that imply that something is both true and false at the same time. But, as for example in the phrase *"our leaders are our children not yet born"* in the poem, these statements have at a deeper level a truthfulness that may be more important than Aristotelian truth.

The symmetric part of bilogic, where every relationship is symmetrical and so can be inverted, is a context dependent logic in which the contexts are constantly changing and overlapping in different ways from one moment to the next. In the dream example, the initial context was that a therapist would be supporting me. So by symmetry I was supporting the therapist (a shift of context). In addition a background context was that I was supporting a friend. So (another shift of context) the friend was the therapist. And the one being supported was "giving birth". So my friend was giving birth ... It is a process of freely shifting images and contexts with its own rich dynamics. A dynamic that owes nothing to the fixed systems of Aristotle.

Once we start thinking in terms of context-dependent logic, a whole new world of ideas opens up, which I want to sketch here. It draws on a debate that has continued for nearly a century about what it means to "prove" something in mathematics.

Let us go back to the difference between Aristotle and Plato regarding proving — the idea of a "theorem", as mathematicians call it. As we have seen, Plato implied that the essence of a theorem was "seeing" that the result was true, while Aristotle probably inclined to the idea that truth was to found by putting together a sequence of logical operations called syllogisms. These two examples illustrate the intuitional and the rational ways of doing things. You might then ask, does each produce the same truths? Certainly there are some things in mathematics that you can reach by Aristotle's rational method of "proof", but which are so complicated that you cannot "see" them, so here Aristotle will score over Plato. But are there some things in mathematics that you can "see" are intuitively true, but which you cannot prove by Aristotle's method? In that case, Plato would score over Aristotle.

More radically, you might go on to ask whether these two approaches really were reaching the same sort of "truth".

By the end of the 19th century mathematicians had come round to thinking that the rational approach was the only possibility. It yielded mathematical truth, and any statement in mathematics that could not be proved in that way was not true. However, the Dutch mathematician L E J Brouwer (born in 1881) strongly argued against this, and his views gave rise to an approach called "intuitionism". Brouwer's ideas were too radical for most of his contemporaries; but his student Arend Heyting developed a compromise approach which allowed proofs whose steps were directly visualisable (even if the net result was not). Brouwer himself never accepted this compromise and called Heyting's work a "sterile exercise".

The most important sort of proof which Heyting and Brouwer rejected is what is called an "indirect proof". In this, you start off by supposing that the result you are trying to prove is *not* true. You then show that, if this were the case, the consequences would be absurd and self-contradictory. So the assumption that the desired result is not true cannot hold. Hence the desired result actually must be true after all! This sort of proof is sometimes called a proof by "reduction to absurdity" (in Latin, *reductio ad absurdum*). It suffers from the drawback that the result is never actually demonstrated in a positive way, so that no way is offered whereby one might intuitively "see" it.

If we represent the result we are trying to prove by R, then the basic assumption of this method is that not "not R" implies R.

In other words, every statement (at least in mathematics) is either true or false and there is nothing in between. This is called "the law of the excluded middle". The distinguishing feature of Heyting's logic is that, though it uses rigorous rational methods, it allows for the possibility of a "middle" between strictly, provably true and strictly, provably false.

Perhaps the most decisive factor in this whole debate was the proof of an astonishing result by the Austrian mathematician Kurt Gödel in 1931 (at the age of 25, one year after finishing his doctorate) concerning the limitations of straight Aristotelian logic, even where indirect, *reductio ad absurdum* proofs are permitted. It showed, to put the essence very simply, that there are statements about numbers (to do with the way prime numbers behave) which *cannot be proved or disproved* from the basic axioms of arithmetic.

The result becomes more extraordinary when one looks at the details. First of all, he did not just consider one particular formulation of arithmetic, but started from the general situation that will hold for *any* rigorous logical system that is sufficiently powerful to handle arithmetic. In other words, there is no limit to the number of extra axioms and methods that one might add to arithmetic: there will still be statements that are not provable or disprovable. Second, his result was direct: he actually specified a procedure which, given a formulation of arithmetic, produced a particular statement which could not be proved. This was a rigorous result: he proved that this formula could not be proved within the given system of arithmetic — but he proved it by using a logical system that was larger and more powerful than the given system. Moreover, his demonstration also proved (in the larger system) that this statement was in fact true.

What is happening here is that the realm of the unprovable will forever outstrip our attempts to grasp it. We can enlarge our systems as often as we like in order to encompass the latest unprovable statements, but there will always be infinitely many new ones waiting over the horizon.

The ideas of Brouwer and Heyting and the theorems of Gödel stand as a "fifth column" within the fortress of rational logic, undermining it from within. In the next chapter we will examine quantum theory and see how it too is governed by a logic that is of the form proposed by Heyting and is context dependent. Our faculty for intuitive reasoning, with its context dependent bilogical structure, is not an unfortunate evolutionary quirk that we must repress and replace with rationality. Rather, it reflects a fundamental structure of the universe. We might speculate that this is why we evolved this intuitive structure in the first place: because it enabled human beings to model and respond to fundamental principles that run through the universe, from the behaviour of atoms to the behaviour of living creatures. This structure, these principles, have found their most explicit expression in the religious traditions that we have examined — in the teachings that lie behind the words of the world's spiritual masters, which still find expression through many modern religious teachers and which infuse the practices of all the major religions. Because of the split that our culture has developed between the intuition and rationality, gross distortions of religion have for millennia been so widespread that it is hard to see the wisdom underneath. But now our awakening to our relationship with the earth provides the ground (literally and metaphorically) on which to rediscover what it is to be truly human.

7

Physics

Greek 'physikos': natural, produced or caused by nature

In a far-off country there was once a mighty king who owned a beautiful vase, fashioned out of the purest rock-crystal. Noblemen came from far and wide to admire the vase. All declared it the most perfect they had ever seen, as they praised the king for his magnificence in possessing such a treasure. But one day a careless steward knocked the vase to the floor, and it split into two pieces.

The king was of course distraught. He sent messengers throughout the land looking for any craftsman or magician who could restore it to its former splendour, offering in reward a tenth of the kingdom; but everyone who was approached declared such a thing to be impossible. The messengers returned and the king went miserably about his doings, until some days later a shabbily dressed young man arrived at the palace demanding an audience. "Your highness," he said in a gentle voice, "I can restore your vase to a state even more beautiful than before." At this the king was outraged. "You mock me," he cried. "I swear that if anyone were to do this he would have half my kingdom and my daughter's hand in marriage. But for your impudence I declare that if you cannot do what you have so rashly promised by tomorrow at noon, you will be put to death."

The next day came and at noon the young man entered and lifted a wrapping from the vase on which he had been working. Seeing it, the king and all the court gasped in amazement. The vase was whole, and in the place where the crack had been there now shone out from within the crystal the most elegant carving of a rose imaginable, completely transforming the crack and making the vase, everyone agreed, even more beautiful than before. The king was happy to reward the young man as he had promised and, needless to say, everyone lived happily ever after.

* * * * *** * * * *

The origin of quantum theory is a bit like the story of the cracked vase. The perfect vase without a flaw is the old physics of Descartes and Newton forged in the seventeenth century. In that theory the universe was seen as completely perfect, like a huge clockwork machine wound up by God at the creation and subsequently ticking predictably away. At any moment each particle in the universe would have a precise speed and position which would determine exactly where it would go next.

We might think of the cracked vase as quantum theory around 1925, at the point when it was realised that Newtonian physics was wrong, and the universe did not have this clockwork perfection. At this point the Danish physicist Niels Bohr introduced as a fundamental principle the condition that speed and position could not both be precise. As a result of this, whenever speed or position was measured the result would be to some extent random, and not determined by a perfect law. Moreover, he proposed, the same held for many other pairs of what he called complementary properties – "complementary" meaning, somewhat confusingly, "exactly incompatible".

The vase with the engraved flower was the fully developed theory that emerged from this, when it was realised that this particular crack is actually the most beautiful element in the whole picture. Without it, electrons would spiral into the nucleus of the atom and matter would collapse. Without it, the fluctuations coming from uncertainty in the initial cosmic fireball that gave rise to the galaxies would never have appeared. In short without it, there would be no universe as we know it.

I am arguing in this book that intuition is the only way in

which we can fully grasp the potential of this crack, and thus any approach to it tends to invoke the numinosity associated with creation and being that we examined in earlier chapters. This means that what was going on at the Solvay conference and what was going on at the Council of Nicaea were closer to each other than anyone has realised. Both were approaching the ultimate mysteries of the universe, and so both had to struggle with integrating the emotions raised by their intuitional side with the need for rational judgement. Now, for the first time for 16 centuries, religion and science have started to come together, not just at a level of superficial similarities of ideas, but at their heart. Just as the power of mystical experience in the past had forced the Council of Nicaea to abandon Aristotelian logic, so the facts of quantum physics forced the delegates at the fifth Solvay conference in 1927 to do the same thing. At Solvay there appeared to be a "crack" in the old logic, and the years that followed were a long struggle to come to terms with this. In this chapter I will focus on the meaning of this "crack" and describe how the revolutionary step of adopting a new logic arose in quantum theory[68].

* * * * *** * * * *

To get a feel for the context of the conference, we can look back to the start of the 20th century. Then physicists still knew almost nothing about the nature of matter. The existence of atoms had been accepted (with some reservations and uncertainty) but no one knew what they were. Electrons had just been discovered, but it was not known whether they were part of the atom, or were freshly produced in some unknown way. It was known[69] that when electricity was discharged through a gas (as in a fluorescent light tube) very precise colours were produced that characterised the gas being used, but there were no clues as to why this was the case. A further puzzle surrounded the reason for the specific blend of colours of the light produced by a hot glowing object, as its temperature increased from red heat to white heat to blue heat.

A particular puzzle had been raised in 1902 by the Hungarian Philipp Lenard who had worked with Hertz (the discoverer of radio waves) at Karlsruhe, Germany. He found that an intense beam of light could pull electrons out of a metal, but that the energy of these electrons did not depend on the intensity of the light. This was incomprehensible on the current theory, which regarded light as a wave of electric and magnetic fields: on that theory, the more intense the light wave was, the more force it would exert on the electrons in the metal, and so the more energy they would have when they were pulled out of the metal.

These mysteries raised issues that stretched back to the 6th century BCE[70]: was the universe basically continuous, like the ocean, or was it basically "discrete": that is, bits and pieces like gravel? Or perhaps it was a mixture, like minestrone? If the universe was like the ocean, then the main pheonomena might be like waves. If it was discrete, they might be like a game of billiards. The solution, if it can be called that, which was emerging from quantum theory at the time of the Solvay conference was, the universe is entirely discrete, like billiard-ball particles, and also it is entirely continuous, like waves!

This perplexing answer emerged in two stages. First of all (in what is sometimes called "old quantum theory") came the idea that electric and magnetic fields, already known to be responsible for light and for radio waves, were not fully continuous, but came in dollops called "quanta". This implied that fields could sometimes behave like particles. The idea was first introduced by a leading German physicist Max Planck as a rather off-beat mathematical trick. But in 1905 Einstein published three revolutionary papers in different fields of physics, and in one of these he proposed that we should take "quanta" more seriously. This started quantum theory as we know it. His careful words do not mention "particle"; he deliberately chooses to place quanta in a state of limbo between wave and particle:

> "According to the assumption considered here, in the production of a light ray emitted from a point source, the energy is not distributed continuously over ever-increasing volumes of space, but consists of a finite number of energy quanta localized at points of space that move without dividing, and can be absorbed or generated only as complete units."

His words, discretely phrased, were groundbreaking. Until then light was thought of purely as a wave in the electric and magnetic fields. In 1801 Thomas Young had apparently demonstrated that light was a wave by shining light through two parallel slits in a screen and getting a pattern of stripes, characteristic of waves, on the other side — a happening called "interference" because the waves interfered with each other, cancelling out in some places and augmenting each other in other places. Now, however, Einstein's "quanta localized at points of space" looked suspiciously like particles, not waves.

Waves and particles were getting disturbingly mixed up. First light, which had been thought a wave, seemed to behave at times like a particle. Next electrons, which had been thought of as particles, seemed to behave as waves, an idea developed in detail in 1925 by Erwin Schrödinger. The idea was confirmed directly in 1927, when Davisson and Germer scattered electrons off a crystal of nickel, where the rows of nickel atoms in the crystal performed the same function as the slits in Young's experiment, and produced the interference pattern characteristic of waves. This idea, of something that was both waves in a continuous field and also, somehow, concentrated like particles (soon to be called "wave-particle duality") was the first of the paradoxes that abounded in quantum theory: a "both/and thinking" that combined incompatible ideas in a way that was forbidden in ordinary logic.

*   *   * * **** *   *   *

The "old quantum theory" introduced by Einstein explained increasingly many findings, including the structure of atoms. Several years earlier Rutherford, working in England, had shown that the atom consisted of a tiny electrically charged nucleus with electrons somehow orbiting around it, even though that was impossibly unstable according to conventional electrical theory. Now Niels Bohr realised that, if one assumed that the energy of the electrons came in quanta, this orbiting was not only made possible, but it also explained the colours of the light that hydrogen emitted when it was heated by an electrical discharge.

At this stage, however, things started to go sour. In the spirit of "quanta" the energy of the electron in hydrogen was not continuously variable, but could only take particular values. Unlike the energy of a beam of light, however, the sizes of the steps in energy, the quanta, were not all the same. A formula had to be used in order to specify how the sizes of the quanta varied. There seemed to be something else going on underneath, that determined the varying sizes of the quanta. Physicists started to realise that the old quantum theory was only a stepping stone to this "something else".

A clue came from looking at the idea of uncertainty, the randomness that seemed to infect atomic events. It was already present in wave-particle duality: a wave was a fuzzy extended object, so when it manifested instead as a particle the particle might appear anywhere in an extended region. Its position was uncertain. Uncertainty also appeared in the characteristic colours of light emitted by hydrogen: the colours were not completely precise, but varied from one moment to the next.

The breakthrough came in 1925. The young German physicist

Werner Heisenberg was struck down by severe hay fever, and in order to recover he retreated to the pollen-free island of Heligoland. Holed up there with no distractions whatever he worked incessantly on these problems and eventually devised a set of mathematical rules that enabled him both to work out the sizes of the quanta for the electrons in atoms, and also the uncertainty in the colour of the light that was emitted. He realised that quantum mechanics was not really about waves versus particles. These were just the two extremes of a trade-off between the uncertainty in the position of an electron and the uncertainty in its momentum (how much impetus a particle delivers when it collides with something): as one decreased, the other increased. Similar trade-offs were responsible for the uncertainty in the colours of emitted light.

Heisenberg publicised his "uncertainty relation" between position and momentum; and a short time later Bohr generalised it into a "complementarity principle" that applied to all physical properties. The crack had been uncovered. Physical properties didn't fit together. To shift the metaphor again, the universe was like a flat-pack from Ikea that had more pieces in it than would actually fit together, the "pieces" being the properties that make up what any particular thing is at given moment. A lot of the time you created good furniture, and didn't need to worry that there was stuff left in the pack. But sometimes you picked up two pieces which obviously didn't fit together snugly: whatever you did they both wobbled a bit (uncertainty). In Bohr's (very confusing) terminology, these were "complementary". A better word would have been "incompatible". Physics had now moved on to the "new quantum theory" or "quantum mechanics", which became the topic of the next Solvay conference , at which Bohr argued that the complementarity principle was the key to a new physics, and the phenomenon of quanta was just a by-product that appeared in particular cases. Most of his colleagues couldn't understand what he was talking about (Ikea, of course, hadn't been invented then).

* * * * *** * * * *

The new physics introduced through complementarity and uncertainty started a profound change in physicists' conceptions of logic and of reality. A feature of this second stage was an emphasis on the process of observation itself. Physicists started to ask, not "what is reality?" but, "how do we observe reality?" Linking reality to particular observations started to bring in the idea that reality depended on the context, as well as the idea that logic depended on the context.

This idea had started earlier with another of Einstein's 1905 papers laying the foundations of relativity. Here, through very simple but ingenious arguments, he showed that basic properties to do with space and time (such as which of two events occurred first) are in many cases not absolute, but context dependent. For example, imagine that two satellites A and B are circling the earth and that each sends out a short radio "bleep", and that both bleeps are received by, say, physicists Robert in New York and Sarah in Paris. Then it could happen that when Robert works out which of the bleeps was transmitted first, making due allowance for the times taken for the bleeps from A and B to reach him, he will conclude that the A-bleep was transmitted before the B-bleep, but when Sarah makes the same calculations she concludes that the order was the other way round. It is not that one of them is "wrong" and the other "right"; rather, the property "before", when referring to a distant event, depends on the context of the physicist making the observations. Apart from the introduction of Robert and Sarah, this is not a contrived example that could never occur in practice: the global positioning system has to cope with this phenomenon every microsecond of the day, and the Satellite Navigation device in your car has to take account of this effect whenever it computes your position.

At first the change in thinking introduced by this idea was

quite subtle. Before Einstein's work, scientists assumed that their subject matter was the absolute reality of the universe, and their task was to observe it without significant experimental bias and then to understand it. After Einstein, there were still many absolutes (part of Einstein's achievement was to introduce new, more robust, absolutes) but some old absolutes lost their status and became context dependent. Physicists now had to be concerned about both experimental bias (error) away from the "real value" and also context dependence which meant that there was no "real value" to look for.

Einstein's work gave a new focus to the status of observation (which does not need to have a human observer, but can be a machine like a Satellite Navigation unit). Deciding whether an aspect of nature is really absolute is not just a philosophical issue; it also requires a careful study of what methods you might use to measure this aspect, and whether they really are independent of context.

Bohr's approach to quantum theory carried this context dependence to a new level. He realised that at the level of very small objects, context dependence dominated everything. Almost any situation offered a choice of optional contexts, where choosing one context ruled out others because the properties involved were complementary (please remember, this means "incompatible"). You could set up your observation to measure position, and that ruled out measuring momentum, and vice versa.

* * * * *** * * * *

Quantum theory matters because (although essentially a part of physics) it points beyond physics to a truly integrated knowing that spans authentic physical science and conscious awareness. Despite claims to the contrary, I believe that we do not as yet have such integration, but a succession of books has now sketched its provisional outlines. Its possibility came to public awareness in the metaphorical approach of Fritjoff Capra's *The Tao of Physics*, and the first steps to a genuinely scientific approach were taken by Roger Penrose in *The Emperor's New Mind*. By now developments in physics and psychology give us strong hints at what such an integration will look like.

To put this in context, let me give an overview of the whole course of quantum theory in the following list, before turning back to its early days. It introduces the key physicists who fomented this revolution.

Old quantum theory: 1905 – 1925/6: Planck 1900; Einstein 1905; Bohr 1913.

... based on the idea that physical quantities like energy were not continuous but came in little dollops called quanta (the plural of quantum).

New quantum theory: 1925/26 – 1981: Heisenberg 1925; Schrödinger 1925, 1926; Eckart 1926; (metaphors underlined by Capra 1975).

... held that quanta were not important: energy was sometimes in quanta and sometimes not. What was important was uncertainty and a strange phenomenon called collapse (p. 125). But the name "quantum" had by this time stuck.

No-collapse quantum theory: 1981 – : Zurek 1981, Zeh 1996; (moves made towards an integrated knowledge by Penrose 1989).

... held that collapse wasn't important either, and might not exist at all. What was important was a much more concrete phenomenon called decoherence.

With this in mind, we can now look more closely at the legacy of the 1927 Solvay conference. The actual debates at the conference were not recorded at the time: we have only fragments from a few letters and later recollections. Much of it was concerned with technical issues of laboratory investigation. But the part of interest here was the discussions between Einstein and Bohr about how to resolve the paradoxes of quantum theory.

As we have seen, Bohr's position was that there is nothing wrong with the concepts of position and momentum in themselves. Indeed, we must hold onto them because they are what physicists understand and they provide a common ground for conversation. But we can no longer apply them without restriction. Just as Einstein had earlier proposed that the measurement of time was not absolute, but the result was relative to the observer, so now Bohr proposed that, in the quantum realm, position and momentum (or waviness and particleness) were even more relative to the observer: it depended on the observer whether or not the particle *even had such a thing as a position or a momentum*. Bohr was thus saying that, depending on the context, there were some propositions like "the position of this electron is 10cm from the edge of the chamber" that are neither true nor false; and so he was implicitly altering logic to being context dependent. In quantum theory the range of questions whose truth could be determined was variable, depending on the observational context. When one carried out an observation of position, then the context changed so that its position existed, but its value was to some extent random, having only a tenuous connection with the previous context.

For Einstein, the idea of something intrinsically random in nature, something without any determining cause, seems to have been abhorrent. Writing 22 years later, Bohr recalled how

Einstein mockingly asked us whether we could really believe that the providential authorities took recourse to dice-playing (". . . ob der liebe Gott würfelt"), to which I replied by pointing at the great caution, already called for by ancient thinkers, in ascribing attributes to Providence in every-day language.[71]

We can note that the participants themselves had some awareness of a connection between their own discussions and former discussions on religious matters, if only at a "mocking" level.

Following the conference, quantum theory began progressively to be made systematic and tidy, but without ever really addressing the fundamental problems that were worrying Einstein. In the course of this the two early equivalent ways of describing a particle — Schrödinger's wave and Heisenberg's collections of numbers — began to be recognised as two different expressions of a single abstract mathematical object which came to be known as a "quantum state".

This concept, around which there are still strong philosophical and scientific disagreements, will play a prominent role in what follows. At the start of the Solvay conference, Schrödinger's approach was much more popular than that of Heisenberg. A wave was something that all physicists were happy with. They could visualise it and they knew how it might behave, and so for a long time there was a desire to hold on to this picture. But in the course of discussion at the conference it was realised that as soon as one moved from describing one particle to describing two particles, the notion of a wave became rather strange. A wave crossing a pool of water is described by specifying how far the surface of the water is above or below its resting level at each point on the surface at a given time. At some points the water is raised and at some points it is lowered. So an ordinary wave depends on position and time. This was essentially still the case also with the wave that Schrödinger introduced in order to describe a single particle such as the electron in a hydrogen atom as it revolves around the nucleus. It was a bit more complicated than a water wave, depending on position in three dimensions rather than in the two-dimensional surface of the pond, and the height of the water was replaced by something more involved which I will call the *amplitude*, but the image of the pond remained fairly reliable.

When it came to describing two particles, however, then the amplitude of Schrödinger's "wave" depended on *two* positions (one for each particle) with three dimensions for each particle, a total of six dimensions. Mathematically this was a minor change, but conceptually it was drastic: the wave was now not a wave in ordinary space, but in a six-dimensional abstract space. The Schrödinger faction wanted to stick to the idea of a wave, though now it began to be called a "wave function" as an indication that it was more than an ordinary wave. The Heisenberg faction, however, protested that it was misleading to call it a wave, and later embraced the terminology of "quantum state", a mathematical object that could be represented either as an amplitude depending on two or more positions in space (though even this became impossible with later developments), or as the matrices of Heisenberg's original approach.

Once aspect of this shift from a wave to a wave-function/quantum state is crucial for what will come in later chapters. An ordinary wave depends on one position and time; it is about the here and now, or as physicists say, it is *local*. The quantum state depends on many positions, bringing together information from positions arbitrarily far away from each other. It is *non-local*, a property that has to do with the unity that we see, and intuit, in the cosmos.

What was happening here was that a key ingredient in physics had moved from the natural realm of things that could be visualised into the realm of Plato's ideas (which included mathematical objects). Deeply divisive at the time, it is this shift from the natural into the Platonic that has made quantum physics difficult ever since. Like Plato's ideas, the quantum state does not "exist" the way a rock or a flower exists. From now on existence becomes an issue, not a platitude. So increasing emphasis came to be placed on the process of observation: one could not assume that anything "is" if one had not observed it to "be". Questions like this had engaged philosophy for centuries, but now they actually had definite physical consequences.

The only "meaning" that the quantum state had, was as a way of prescribing the probabilities for getting different various possible outcomes to measurements (observations) on the particle. It was realised that if one performed the same observation twice running on a particle with minimal time between the two observations, the second observation was no longer random: it had to agree with the first observation. So the first observation altered the probabilities for observations, and hence altered the quantum state. The many probabilities "collapsed" into a single certainty. Thus was born the idea of the "collapse of the quantum state" (or collapse of the wave-function, using Schrödinger's earlier language).

In retrospect, Bohr and Einstein had presented the world of physics with two alternatives (neither of them fully grasped at the time) and the world of physics had rejected both of them and adopted a third alternative. Bohr had been implicitly suggesting a new logic that was context dependent. Einstein had been suggesting the need for a wholly new set of concepts to replace position, momentum and the like; but he was unable to discover what these were, and much of the later part of his life was spent in a fruitless search for them. Physicists, by and large, opted for a "two worlds" solution. There was the Platonic quantum world, ruled by the quantum state, which for most of the time evolved predictably according to precise (though somewhat unfamiliar and complicated) physical laws and was rather like a wave. And there was the classical world which they were already familiar with, containing large laboratory objects that for most of the time also followed predictable, but familiar, laws. Every so often the two worlds collided, so to speak, in an "observation", at which point each world was jerked randomly into a new path, according to laws that were only statistical and not predictable.

Historically this picture worked satisfactorily for a while, but it has become untenable for one very basic reason. Observations, of the sort envisaged by physicists, take place in physics laboratories; but most of the universe, and most of our planet, does not consist of physics laboratories. This becomes a particularly acute problem in cosmology. Here we now have strong evidence that the very early universe was almost completely smooth and uniform, but today it is of course very lumpy indeed! The evidence from observations using satellites show that fluctuations away from uniformity arose very early on and grew to produce the galaxies and eventually ourselves. Moreover, these fluctuations appear to have the same form as do the fluctuations due to quantum effects that appear in, for example, the light of a laser when it is observed. In other words, the structure of the universe seems to arise from quantum fluctuations. As one commentator put it, "the galaxies are quantum fluctuations writ large across the sky." But such fluctuations can only come out of a smooth, symmetrical state through an observation, and the very early universe, with its almost complete uniformity, is as far from containing anything like a physics laboratory as can be imagined. Some might be tempted to invoke God here as a universal observer, but this crude solution would be a misunderstanding of both God and physics. The only possibility seems to be some version of a proposal by John Wheeler: the "observations" that bring into being these fluctuations are those being made *now* by innumerable systems and organisms which are themselves the products of the fluctuations which they produce. The universe "pulls itself up by its own bootstraps" with the later structure creating, through action that is apparently going backwards in time, the conditions for its own existence. This proposal of Wheeler's lines up with his parable about the origin of being which I described in Chapter 6. Though (as far as I know) he never brought these two together in this explicit way, it would seem that he felt that the problem of being, how the actual universe arises, why "there is something rather than nothing", is to be found in the act of observation — but one still remaining mysterious because of its looping back in time. And observation has this creative property because of complementarity, because of the crack (the wobble in the Ikea parts) which leaves open what is going to emerge next.

A further problem with the idea of observation is present even in conventional physics. Imagine a laboratory physics experiment, in which, for example, a fast electron is emitted by a radioactive atom placed inside a chamber equipped with apparatus to detect it (see the diagram below). The electron passes through the air in the chamber, knocking other electrons off the atoms that it passes; charged electrical plates then accelerate these many electrons which in turn release other electrons from more atoms, giving a whole cascade of electrons, which adds up to a significant pulse of electricity when it arrives at one of the plates. This pulse is then amplified by electronics and the information stored in a computer record, which is subsequently displayed and inspected by a physicist.

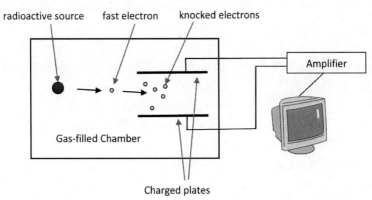

Schematic representation of a typical observation in quantum physics. The passage of a single fast particle is amplified and recorded.

The question is, when does the "observation" take place? Was it when the particle made the trail of electrons? Or when the trail had been amplified by the electronics in a large pulse of electric current? Or when this pulse was recorded in the computer? Or when the display was recorded in turn by the eyes and visual brain area of the physicist? Or when the physicist finally became conscious of the outcome of the whole laboratory process? When this debate first arose, the physicist Eugene Wigner held to this latter view that in quantum theory consciousness itself could have physical effects. The majority, however, held to the view that an observation had occurred once a large-scale event, like the amplified pulse of electricity in the equipment, had occurred.

To this day, Wigner's view has remained in the minority, but it is this idea that has fuelled excitement over quantum theory ever since. If our conscious thoughts or perceptions can influence physical reality, not by mechanical interactions but by the mere fact that they become conscious, then a whole mass of religious ideas starts to look more credible. Perhaps praying for particular events could indeed cause them to happen. Perhaps God really is a super-observer carrying out observations on the entire universe. I have to warn readers that I will have to quash ideas as crude as this, which are at variance with the actual facts of how matter behaves. But, as we will see later, these ideas do carry a germ of truth. We will see in chapter 8 that the outcome of an observation is influenced not just by the situation close to the apparatus, but by the situation in the entire cosmos, expressed through a version of the quantum state that is outside space and time. It is the cosmos as a single unity that enters into this creative act that brings a definite outcome from the opportunity presented by the crack of uncertainty. So there is a real link between quantum theory and the notion of unity that, as we have seen, is so important in religion. And so it is quantum uncertainty, together with unity, that enables love, the other characteristic of religion, to have effect.

Two important developments in physics have had a large influence on the above argument. The first was work by John von Neumann which showed that in fact it didn't matter how one answered the questions listed above about where the observation took place: the results would be exactly the same wherever it was, provided that it happened in a system that was sufficiently large to behave in an essentially classical way. The second development was a criterion for what this "sufficiently large" actually was. The essential difference between quantum behaviour and classical behaviour is that quantum behaviour can have a wave aspect, and a wave has a *phase:* you are at the crest of the wave, or the trough, or halfway down ... A system behaves quantum mechanically if all its parts have phases that are in step; such a system is called *coherent.* The bigger a system is, the harder it is for the parts to stay coherent, because any system, whether the electronics in the apparatus or the nerve cells in the physicist's brain, is constantly being disturbed by the heat-vibrations that affect all systems on earth, unless they are super-cooled in a laboratory. It is this *decoherence* that marks the point where an "observation" takes place, in the sense of the term used by physicists.

The notion of decoherence has revolutionised our understanding of quantum theory. The mysterious notion of the "collapse of the quantum state" which dominated quantum theory for so long, and posed so many problems, has now been replaced by the entirely explicable phenomenon of decoherence, producing what many authors are now calling "no collapse quantum theory". This picture then has fascinating implications for biology, because biological systems have evolved to control quantum phenomena as closely as possible, so as to extract the last scrap of energy from their internal processes. The question now becomes, to what extent can a biological system stave off the transition to a classical system? A system that could behave like a quantum computer would have great evolutionary advantages, and some (including myself) are convinced that this can happen, through indirect mechanisms, in elongated systems as large as human neurons.

*   *   *   * *** *   *   *   *

In the previous chapter I described the extraordinary changes that took place in the study of logic during the twentieth century at the hands of mathematicians such as Brouwer and Gödel, and the bilogic of Matte Blanco which offers the possibility of a logic that applies to intuition. A natural question is, how do these relate to quantum theory?

The idea that quantum theory requires a new sort of logic goes back to 1936 when the mathematicians Garrett Birkhoff and John von Neumann[72] pointed out that the structure of the mathematics of quantum theory was roughly the same as the structure of logic, leading them to recast the mathematics in a form that they called "quantum logic". After some years, however, it became clear that this quantum logic was so unlike ordinary logic that the name was misleading. While the reformulation gave insight into what was going on in quantum theory, it did not really get to grips with the way in which logic was being bent by quantum theory. More than this was needed in order to understand what was happening at the level of logic.

To progress further, we need to look more deeply at what it is that is "odd" about quantum theory. So far we have talked about complementarity, which is to do with the way different properties interfere with each other when you try to measure them, and wave-particle duality in which physical "things" sometimes appear as particles and sometimes as waves. We might agree that this sort of behaviour is odd, but is it strictly illogical? The impossibility of measuring properties, as a result of complementarity, might be frustrating if you are a physicist, but perhaps physicists simply have to get used to not knowing everything. The philosopher of quantum mechanics Bernard d'Espagnat has coined the phrase "veiled reality" for this restriction on what can be known. So far, then, it could be the case that nature is behaving perfectly logically "behind the scenes" but without our being able to observe it.

The evidence that there is more to it than this, and that we really do need to alter logic, comes from a result proved in 1967 by Simon Kochen from Princeton University and Ernst Specker from the prestigious technical institute ETH Zurich. To explain their result, we need to take stock of what we can know at a given time about some particular system, such as an atom or a particle going round and round in an accelerator, and what might be going on behind the scenes. For any such system there will be a range of properties, each one of which can be measured separately if we wish — properties such as position, energy, momentum or angular momentum (the impetus of spinning that an ice-skater, for instance, uses in performing fast turns). While some pairs of properties cannot be measured at the same time, many pairs of properties can, and so physicists can discover many relationships that always hold between certain pairs of properties by measuring them at the same time. An example of a pair of properties might be the angular momentum of a particle for its rotation about some particular axis, and the total angular momentum of the particle: the total is never less than the angular momentum about any particular axis.

What Kochen and Specker showed was that, for *any* quantum system except the simplest of all (an electron at rest) it was not logically possible for all the properties of the system to have values which satisfied all the relations that were known to hold between them. In other words, they proved rigorously that it was not just your own incompetence that stopped the parts in the flat-pack from fitting together, but that there was no possible way of fitting them together. Yet another way of expressing this is to say that not only can we not *observe* the values of all the properties at once, but the system cannot *logically have* the values of all its properties at once. So there is an issue in logic here: the context dependence of quantum mechanics, which requires different contexts in which observe different properties, extends to a context dependence of the logic of quantum mechanics, in which the truth or falsity of statements about the system depends on context — and in some contexts it will be the case that some statements are neither true not false.

Of course, this is just the sort of thing we are used to in everyday life and everyday speech: some contexts cannot be mixed, as illustrated by the phrase, much valued in our household, "looking for verbs in the refrigerator"[73]. Since the time of Newton, however, science had supposed that the physical account of the universe as a collection of particles moving according to eternal laws was an ultimate context that was always applicable, providing an absolute logical foundation for reality.

In 1998 the mathematical physicist Chris Isham and the philosopher of science Jeremy Butterfield[74] realised that the situation which Kochen and Specker had highlighted was exactly suited to a new branch of mathematics first developed in 1969 called topos theory[75]. It belongs to a wider area of mathematics called category theory which explores mathematics in terms of the sort of processes and logical structures that are involved, rather than in terms of the sorts of mathematical objects that are being handled. From this point of view, the important thing about a system of logic is that the classification into TRUE or FALSE acts as a process for restricting the possible scope of the current situation. The definition of a topos formalises and generalises this requirement. In practical applications, this means that topos logic is context dependent and "truth" is not something that takes two values, but can be a much broader process of classification.

Isham and Butterfield linked this to the Kochen Specker theorem via the idea of "coarse graining": replacing a rather precise property by a more broadly based one. For example, the position of a particle to the nearest centimetre is a coarse graining of its position to the nearest millimetre. A coarse grained observation is compatible with more observations than a fine grained one, and one can derive the Kochen Specker result by examining the connections that exist between different coarse grainings of properties. Instead of a "truth function" which simply classifies all statements about properties into TRUE or FALSE, their topos logic for quantum theory has a "truth object" which, for each context, supplies for each set of statements about properties the extent to which the properties have to be coarse grained in order to make the statements valid. The hard and fast "TRUE or FALSE" is replaced by a blurred "yes, if you three-quarters close your eyes".

I have described this development because it indicates how rigorous mathematical physics is now introducing genuinely logical notions that start to make sense of quantum theory. But I would argue that this work is still missing the point, in that it is still ignoring the intuitive side of the universe and of our minds. As well as altering the formal structure of logic, we need to recapture the qualitatively different way in which Plato's *alētheia* (unveiling) went beyond the purely rational. This is achieved by Matte Blanco's bilogic because it is derived from the workings of the unconscious, even though it can be expressed in formal and rigorous terms.

There are similarities between topos logic and bilogic which are fruitful for future development. Coarse graining involves a "lumping together", as does the behaviour of the unconscious and the association of ideas which, as I will describe later[76], Farhad Dalal identified as the crucial dynamic of our use of language. In terms of Matte Blanco's logic, these are examples of "the part is the same as the whole". The lumping by association that we see in the intuitional mind is, of course, very different in kind from the coarse graining by numerical averaging that is characteristic of Isham and Butterfield's approach. But they are sufficiently similar to suggest strongly that our intuitional/ rational polarity has evolved in response to the fundamental crack in the universe on which Bohr laid so much stress. There is a basis here for working towards an understanding of this crack at a deeper level, which can give rise both to quantitative aspects of quantum theory and the qualitative behaviour of our minds which are attuned to a cracked world.

We saw earlier how poetry can make explicit use of this process, and I now recall a verse of Laurie Lee's poem "April Rise" which makes explicit the way in which words and concepts can be drawn together by the affinities of association:

> Pure in the haze the emerald sun dilates,
> The lips of sparrows milk the mossy stones,
> While white as water by the lake a girl
> Swims her green hand among the gathered swans. [77]

Here the meanings of the words spread like pools beyond their printed bounds, merging towards a dynamic coarse-graining over a constantly changing context.

It is only our obsessive over-emphasis on the rational that has caused us to forget this dynamism of the intuitive. We have developed physical science to the extent that we have because it has seemed a refuge from the anarchy of the intuitive, retreating to the comfort (for some!) of rigorous science. And yet even here the twofold nature of our world has appeared.

The human organism has evolved to match the nature of the world in a particular way, opening a particular window on the world. Being true to this window is what it is to be human, and this involves recognising its twofold nature. It is salutary to realise from the example of quantum theory that this world is one and cannot be divided up. When we attempt to do so, as was done for the last three centuries of shunning the intuitive, eventually the shunned component shows up in a logical disguise, reminding us that we should have been taking it into account all along.

8

Field and Inchoate

Field: a state or situation in which a force is exerted on any objects of
a particular kind (e.g. electric charges) that are present
Inchoate: imperfect, undeveloped ... Latin — incohare (to begin)

We can now start pulling our themes together, ready to encounter in the chapter after next the god Pan whom we first met in Chapter 2, to lead us to our goal of an ecological vision. In this chapter I want to pin down the meaning of "Quantum". What is it really about? What has it got to do with religion? How does it affect the daily living of us humans? And what is the place of this mysterious "field" on which much has been written recently?

First, let me quickly recap the last few chapters. In Chapter 6 we became aware of the mystery of *being,* and we looked at it from several sides. We considered how Plato had presented the mystery in terms of a meeting between the "ideas" (*eidōn*), and "space" (*chora*). The "idea" corresponded to form while *chora* corresponded to matter; and somehow concrete particular being was supposed to emerge from these two. We also looked at "being" from the perspective of the mystic, for whom being was both the ultimate divinity, and also our own inner essence. Then in Chapters 7 and 8 we traced the boomerang-like history of logic: which started with Plato's vision of truth as the unveiling of mystery; turned to continue with science into greater levels of intellectual abstraction; turned again with the arrival of quantum physics when scientists started to become aware of the limitations of logic; and turned further to encounter the quantum phenomenon of complementarity that marked out the limits of logic.

In the last chapter we described how the "crack" of complementarity left open what actually came into existence as a result of a quantum process, what actually *becomes*. And as we shall see later, this emergence, this mystery of being, involves an interplay between the unity of the whole cosmos and the particular context. So the history of logic finally approached its original starting point with a suggestion that complementarity could contain the mystery of being. In these chapters we realised that, in order to navigate this emerging vision of the world, we needed repeatedly to bring together our two faculties of thought: rationality and intuition. It was only intuition that could darkly know the place of *being*, between *eidōn* and *chora*.

In this chapter we come up to date. In contemporary physics the "idea" – precise, rational, eternal – becomes the "quantum field", while *chora* becomes the "quantum state", with indirect links to the process of being and the intuitive or numinous. I want to provide here a rough sketch of these two central notions of physics. In previous chapters I have reached quantum concepts by following the often tortuous paths taken by the history of quantum theory, as physicists struggled to change their thinking, step by step, from nineteenth century "classical" physics to twentieth century quantum physics. But today there is a quicker path, which I shall use here: a mental teleportation that carries us in a single leap from a nineteenth century classical field to a twentieth century quantum field. This teleport is called "quantisation".

But one word of warning: many books have depicted the quantum field as wonderful, non-local, mystical, creative, all-powerful ... Some of this arises from confusion with the quantum state, some of it arises from confusion with God. So I ask for your patience. The mystery of being will be found to lie more deeply than the quantum field.

* * * * **** * * * *

To apply the magic of quantisation physicists start with the older concept of a classical field. I will take the magnetic field as an example, something many will know from playing with a magnet. When you do so, the first thing you discover is that there is a vaguely defined region around the magnet, extending perhaps up to a dozen centimetres, within which iron or steel objects are "grabbed" and drawn towards it. Michael Faraday, the pioneer of the science of electricity and magnetism, in the 1840s, referred to this region as the "magnetic field", using the word in the same rather general sense as when one talks of the "field of view" out of a window.

As you explore further, this region starts to show more detailed properties. If you place a sheet of paper over a magnet, and sprinkle over it tiny scraps of iron, "iron filings", the result is an elegant array of curved lines. If you were to place a small compass at any point in this picture, you would find that these lines ran in the direction in which the compass points.

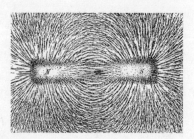

The pattern formed when iron filings are sprinkled over a sheet of paper resting over a bar-magnet.

Phenomena like this tend to make one think in terms of some sort of invisible structure surrounding the magnet which the filings make visible. Faraday soon thought the same: by 1850 he was talking about "fields of force in which the lines of magnetic power would vary". At that time some physicists may have thought in terms of a physical substance surrounding magnets and electrical circuits. But they were cautious about taking this too literally. The Scottish physicist James Clerk Maxwell, who established the final version of the mathematical laws of these phenomena, pointed out that the effects discovered by Faraday could be accounted for by swirling motions inside the atoms surrounding electrical conductors; but he also warned that such an approach could be a distraction, and that what one should be seeking was a "mode of connexion existing in nature"[78] not an artificial attempt to produce a mechanical explanation. Throughout the 19th century, the idea of a "field" provided this explanation. It was a sort of hybrid object, more physical that just a mathematical abstraction, but less concrete than the Newtonian matter that was supposed to make up atoms.

The discoveries that I have sketched for the magnetic field were repeated for the electric field, and then a combined theory of the "electromagnetic field" was developed by Maxwell which described the interaction between the two, including the revolutionary discovery of radio waves.

I will follow this history a little further in order to motivate the idea of quantisation. As quantum theory was developed in the 1920s, it became obvious that the theory would have to be extended to include the electromagnetic field. For instance, as we noted in the previous chapter, one of the driving problems for quantum theory had been the question of why an atom is stable. At the start of the twentieth century it was known that the hydrogen atom consisted of a single electron with a negative electric charge and a small heavy nucleus with an opposite positive charge, and it was supposed that the electron orbited round the nucleus like the earth round the sun, the two being attracted by their opposite electric charges. But the electrically charged electron moving round in its orbit constituted a varying electric current, which according to Maxwell's theory should have generated radio waves, which should in turn have dissipated energy, causing the electron to spiral into the nucleus and merge with it in a fraction of a second. No more hydrogen! Quantum theory supplied most of the answer to the problem: the electron could only loose energy, and the electromagnetic field could only gain energy, in discrete dollops called "quanta", so that there could be no gradual leaking away of energy; but there was no proper theory about how the electrically charged electron and the electromagnetic field interacted at the quantum level. What was the full quantum story about the generation of radio waves?

So the problem was, given a well understood classical theory (such as Maxwell's equations for electromagnetism) which was known to work well for large objects (like a coil of wire) what do you have to do in order to transform it into the corrected quantum version that would also work for small systems (like the hydrogen atom)? This transformation is quantisation. The core of the answer was provided in 1926 by the German physicist Pascual Jordan, along with Werner Heisenberg, whom we met in the last Chapter, and the mathematician Max Born. In a succession of papers they laid the foundations for how one quantises a field, like the electromagnetic field. At the same time Paul Dirac at the University of Cambridge, England, was putting the whole process of quantisation onto a firm footing. Later on a succession of mathematical problems emerged with this method, which has occupied the physics community ever since, but initially the results seemed to provide a clear solution to the problem of the stability of the atom.

"Classical" means, in this context, to do with the physics started by Newton and continuing up to the twentieth century. It deals very well with systems ranging from balls rolling down slopes, spinning gyroscopes or the solar system consisting of the sun and the planets, to waves on a pond or electric coils producing radio waves. There is a technical difference between the first of these examples and the last. A rolling ball or a simplified model of the solar system can be described by a finite number of quantities. (For the solar system these would be the positions of all the planets and the sun together with their speeds and directions of motion.) Systems involving waves or fields, on the other hand, which are spread out continuously in space, would require an infinite set of quantities to specify them. An important stage in the development of quantisation was the realisation that, though there is a technically important difference between systems based on finitely many properties and on infinitely many, conceptually all these classical systems are on the same footing.

The key concepts for quantising a system, whether its description is finite or infinite, are "state" and "property". At any given moment in time a classical system has a state: a specification, as complete as possible, of the state-of-affairs at that time. The classical system has a variety of different properties that depend on the state. For the solar system the positions of the planets are typical properties, but there are also more general properties like the total energy of the system. In classical physics (but, as we shall see, not in quantum physics) once you know the state you can work out what are the values of all the properties, and vice versa.

The classical state is a collection of numbers, but it also describes a concrete physical state of affairs. Quantisation will take the mathematical aspect of the classical state as a category of mathematical objects and by, altering the mathematical properties of this category, will produce quantum states. But in doing this is will lose the concrete interpretation of the state.

At this stage things get a bit technical, so I am going to jump to the end of the story now, and put a few more details in the next section. The answer to "what is a quantum field?" is "an algebra that represents the extent to which the defining properties of a (classical) system are complementary." I realise that this definition is probably unhelpful. (For most readers it is probably about as helpful as the answer "42" which came as the Answer to the Ultimate Question of Life, the Universe, and Everything in *The Hitch Hiker's Guide to the Universe*.) To unpack it a little ... A quantum field is a purely abstract mathematical object. It is not a here-and-now field like the classical field of a particular magnet on a particular table, but an encoding of the basic properties of any possible actual field of a given type. It is defined as a structure filling the entire universe and expressing the properties of the field in complete (but abstract) detail.

In modern quantum theory an actual field of a particular magnet, or whatever is producing it, is given by the quantum state, which we met in the last chapter. Like Plato's *eidōs*, a quantum field is the prerequisite for any actual field in the form of a quantum state. So the connection between the quantum field and, say, the real magnetic field of the earth, is very much the same as the connection between Plato's "idea" of a horse and an actual horse. Plato's idea of a horse is a sort of blue-print for an actual horse, and the quantum field is a sort of blue-print for constructing any particular actual field. The similarity with a blue-print should not be pushed too far, however. An architect's blue-print depicts one particular building in a highly reduced form: in two dimensions rather than three, in lines rather than bricks, in centimetres rather than metres. The quantum field is thought of as providing the rules for *any* actual field of a given type, not just one particular instance; as being spread out at full scale in space and time; and as containing the maximum specifiable detail for the physics of the field concerned.

Being spread out in space and time, both the classical field and the quantum field are *local*, unlike the quantum state. They are both essentially mechanical concepts, in the sense that Faraday and his successors understood this: namely, satisfying good, old-fashioned physical principles. When one part of a field changes, it gives the adjacent part a shove, so that it changes, and then it shoves the next, so that a ripple spreads out like a disturbance in the water in a pond. A mathematical version of these mechanical principles is faithfully reproduced in the quantum field. The quantum field is non-specific (it does not describe a particular field of a particular magnet), but completely definite; the state is specific, but veiled, ideal and expressing potentiality.

While the quantum field is local, the quantum state is, as I have already described, *not* local. The mathematical shift described in the next section is not the only change which quantisation makes to the classical situation: the notion of the "state" also changes. In the classical case, as I remarked earlier in connection with the solar system, the state is specified by all the relevant positions of the parts of the system together with their rates and directions of change, but in the quantum case specifying all this information is forbidden by the uncertainty principle. In this case, the state specifies the *probability* that a particular property or set of properties will be found to have a particular value when measured[79]. Because the quantum state deals in probabilities, it can encode statistical correlations between properties over great distances. This is the sense in which the quantum state is non-local. It is the basis for the "spooky action at a distance" which so worried Einstein in the years following the Solvay conference.

The quantum state and the quantum field form a sort of polarity that sets a framework within which actuality emerges. The quantum state summarises the possibilities and probabilities for what might emerge and manifest in the particular present set circumstances. The quantum field describes the physical properties that must shape the way the quantum state changes and must govern and constrain its probabilities. But neither of these in themselves causes manifestation. We go back to John Wheeler's parable in Chapter 6: the physicist can spread out her equations on the table, but the universe does not spring into life. *Being* is to be found at a deeper level than state or field, and that, as we have seen, is the province of intuition, which is tapped (not always successfully) by religion. This is part of what is expressed by the image and the message of spirit flying into the arms of matter in chapter 6.

* * * * *** * * * *

In this section, which is not essential to what comes after it, I will enlarge in more detail on the quantum field. In the last chapter we saw how very different quantum theory and classical theory are as regards states and properties. According to Bohr, a quantum system does not actually *have* properties in the way that a classical system does. Instead, properties correspond to carrying out some particular measuring experiment; he claimed that they do not exist apart from the process of measurement. In addition Bohr introduced the principle of "complementarity" (properties interfering with one another) that determines the details of a distinctive context dependent logic (the topos logic examined in the last chapter) for quantum propositions.

Quantisation is about how to build a theory about a very small (quantum) version of a classical system. This was the problem that faced physics at the start of the twentieth century when it was proposed that the atom was a tiny version of the solar system, with the nucleus as the sun and the electrons as the planets, and at that time the solution had to be found through many years of frustrating trial and error. Quantisation achieves the same thing by focussing on complementarity, the key step being to determine which pairs of classical properties will become complementary in the quantum version. In the case of a simple system such as two particles moving in an orbit round each other (like the hydrogen atom) complementary properties are things like the angular position of the particles and the corresponding "angular momentum" which we met in the last chapter. In quantum theory a position and its corresponding momentum are complementary. This information needed to construct a quantum version of a classical theory is a specification of which properties will interfere with each other, and by how much, and this can be done purely by examining the mathematics of the classical system. Following this realisation, physicists now apply the word "complementary" to classical properties whose quantum versions are complementary in Bohr's sense.

There are many different ways of presenting the information about complementarity: the commonest one involves constructing a mathematical structure called an *algebra*[80] out of all the properties. In an algebra properties can be added and multiplied together, but using a fancy form of multiplication in which $a \times b$ is usually different from $b \times a$.

One distinction that should be borne in mind here is the distinction between the *concept* of a property, which is a Platonic "idea", and the *value* of that property for some state, which is a number that relates to a particular existing system, here and now. For classical systems the distinction seems pedantic, but it becomes important when quantising, to create a quantum version. When you multiply numbers together the order does not matter; so when you multiply the values of properties together the order does not matter. But for the quantum field the conceptual properties themselves (not their values) are represented as entities whose multiplication depends on the order. When a and b are complementary, $a \times b$ and $b \times a$ differ by Planck's constant. When a and b do not interfere with each other, only then are $a \times b$ and $b \times a$ equal.

Heisenberg's realisation, during his retreat in Heligoland in 1925, that he needed $a \times b$ to be different from $b \times a$ came as quite a shock to him: although mathematicians had used systems like this for a long time, it was new to physicists. He wrote later:

"It was about three o'clock at night when the final result of the calculation lay before me. At first I was deeply shaken. I was so excited that I could not think of sleep. So I left the house and awaited the sunrise on the top of a rock."[81]

In the course of the development of this idea by Heisenberg, and later with Jordan and Born, an intriguing possibility emerged. Schrödinger had already produced a formulation of quantum theory in which the behaviour of a particle was determined by a "wave function"; and the wave function behaved in a way that looked rather like the electromagnetic field. So what would happen if one took Schrödinger's wave function and treated it in the same way as electromagnetism had been treated; in other words, if one quantised the particle *again?* The result was that one obtained the quantum theory for a collection of many particles. This was a further twist to the mysterious duality of waves and particles: electromagnetism was classically a wave, but it could be quantised and then was found also to behave like particles; electrons were classically particles, but when they were quantised they behaved like waves. And now what was at first called "second quantisation" produced a quantum theory for a collection of an indefinite number of particles.

It took a while to sort out what seemed a very confusing situation. For instance, was there a "third quantisation" that produced something different again? Fortunately the answer was, no. But after more sorting out, with more help from Paul Dirac, a picture emerged that was clear in outline — although a lot of devils were concealed in the details. The new picture of quantum phenomena was called "quantum field theory", and it has been the basis of most of quantum theory ever since (until the start of modern attempts to incorporate gravity and drive out the devils from the details).

The *quantum field* is essentially the animal that you get when you quantise a field theory like electromagnetism once, or quantise the electron twice. So the quantum field not only underlies what were classically regarded as fields, but it also underlies what were classically regarded as particles.

146

*   *   * * **** *   *   *   *

May I remind you of my goal here, as expressed in my title "weaving the cosmos"? It is to describes a new enterprise for humanity, a story and a technology that brings together the intuitive and the relational as a creative response to the environmental challenge. In this marriage of our faculties each mirrors the other. Our rational concepts can include an accurate concept of intuition (though not its reality), while our intuition can include a qualitative grasp of rationality (though without its precision). So we can inquire what in modern physics might mirror the categories of being and spirit in our intuitive knowing. So far we have only tentative models, usually not in the mainstream. So I would like at this stage to introduce Frederick Parker-Rhodes, a remarkable independent thinker in physics and philosophy who died in 1987. I knew him in the 1970s, when my wife, accompanied by our son of about 18 months, was working part time for a small independent research team called the Cambridge Language Research Unit. The team was both socially and scientifically radical. The grounds of the unit accommodated two roomy wooden garden sheds/chalets. Both provided office space, one for an individual whose productivity was probably impaired by his (rather obvious) drink problem, while the other was occupied by Frederick and his dog. All three were provided at intervals with large mugs of tea (the dog had his in a bowl). The atmosphere and the ideas fostered in the unit had much in common with the picture I am presenting here. A person's essential being was more important than their life-style; and ideas, whether about religion or science, were judged by their content and not by the academic status of those who proposed them.

Frederick's major work, *The Theory of Indistinguishables*, was published in 1981. Its first impression on me, on opening its pages and leafing through in order to get oriented, was that it was the most original book I had ever seen. Usually when reading a book one can spot the strands of thought that have contributed to it directly or indirectly: perhaps philosophical ideas from Plato, or esoteric knowledge from the Hermetic writings, or branches of mathematics that are no longer current. Usually the mathematical notation might be familiar, the terminology might be taken from standard scientific works, the style of argument from a known philosophical source. *The Theory of Indistinguishables*, however, seems to have no family background. Only slowly does one start to recognise in it the occasional familiar face, though in unfamiliar guise.

His starting point does lie in conventional science, where it is well known that the members of each type of fundamental particle are indistinguishable. No two electrons can be distinguished from each other, nor two protons. This is at first hard to grasp. With two identical twins, you know that there are differences between them (at least they themselves know which is which): it is just that you yourself can't discern any difference. But with two electrons there are literally no differences at all. Hence it does not make sense to say that two electrons have changed place, since after what might have been an interchanging of the two, everything is in fact exactly the same as it was before.

This alters all the statistical calculations that one does in physics, because such calculations depend on counting the number of different ways in which things can be arranged, which in turn depends on whether interchanging two of the things does or does not make a difference.

For example, consider the number of ways of arranging three marbles in three boxes, one in each. If the marbles are distinguishable, then we can notionally label them (number 1 is the one with a green fleck on the surface, number 2 ... etc). Then there are three boxes in which number 1 can go, after which there are two remaining boxes where number 2 can go, and that fixes where number 3 goes, so there are 2 x 3, i.e. 6 ways of arranging them. But if the marbles are not distinguishable, then there is only one way of arranging them (namely, a marble in the first box, a marble in the second box, and a marble in the third box). On hearing this argument, most people don't consider it valid. My reaction at first was to insist that they were still different marbles, even if you didn't actually have means of distinguishing them, and so there must still be 6 arrangements. But when you examine the statistics experimentally, you find that tiny particles really do behave as if they were genuinely indistinguishable. The consequences of this are very important. It is the reason, for instance, why matter is solid and it is the basis of phenomena like superconductivity.

Frederick realised that a new sort of logic was at play here. It was a kind of "symmetric logic", but one quite different from that of Matte Blanco (Chapter 6). Like Matte Blanco's however, it was a context dependent logic. You could only discern that you had more than one electron present if the electrons were presented within a single closely defined context. This led him to his most radical step: in order to handle this context-dependent logic, he use a context-dependent mathematical notation, in which the meaning of any symbol changed according to the grammatical context defined by the adjacent symbols. The result is rather like the game of croquet in Lewis Carol's *Alice in Wonderland,* in which the mallets are live flamingos which keep changing their shape whenever you try to make a shot.

Like Matte Blanco's "bilogic" this system admits several different layers of symmetry. In a later unpublished manuscript called *The Wheel of Creation* he describes how, as one passes to smaller and smaller fundamental entities of physics, their features become fewer and fewer, and one can say less and less about them, until almost all distinguishing features have disappeared. Moreover, as one passes to higher and higher non-physical organisational principles of the universe, the layers traditionally described in terms of angels and archangels, we again leave behind the idiosyncratic features that distinguish material beings and move towards the unity that is stressed by mystics, arriving at a state which also lacks almost all distinguishing features. Frederick Parker-Rhodes proposes that the state reached by tracing back to more and more fundamental layers of physics, and the state reached by tracing deeper and deeper mystical insights, are in fact one and the same. He calls this level the *inchoate.*

In *The Theory of Indistinguishables* Frederick derives the basic structures of the universe starting from the inchoate. Its structure is the minimal imaginable: a "twinness" (a notion of not-one, but without any "this" or "that" or "how many") which inevitably carries with it the possibility of difference between oneness and twinness. Hence, argues Parker-Rhodes, as soon as you admit one and more-than-one, there is already implicit a sort of threeness about this level, but no concept of ordinary number, place or existence. In the prologue to *The Wheel of Creation* he tells in mythical form how the universe unfolds from this seed, as if there were three sisters, asleep at the bottom of the ocean, each one dreaming the other two, and the three dreaming the world into existence.

On the side of physics there flows from the inchoate the threeness of the dimensions of space, then the patterns that generate the values of the fundamental constants of nature, and eventually the quantum field. The conundrums that occupied the Solvay conference flow in this manner from their source in the inchoate.

On side of the higher structures of being, there flows from the inchoate the threeness that preoccupied the Council of Nicaea: the intuition that there was a state which combined the essence of unity with the first dawnings of creation and diversity, which, on the Christian way of thinking, found expression in the idea of the Trinity.

What Parker-Rhodes was doing was, and is, deeply unfashionable. He was trying to show that both the aspects of the universe that we classify as "physical" and the aspect that we classify as "spiritual" stem from one single fundamental origin, the inchoate. And, to make it even more unfashionable, in *The Inevitable Universe* (another unpublished manuscript) he claims that the nature of this fundamental origin can be discovered purely by rational inquiry. As philosophers put it, it is an *a priori* principle rather than something deduced from observation. Personally I cannot accept the whole of this claim. The details of Parker-Rhodes' system have some uncertainty in terms of mathematical rigor. Moreover intuition is involved as well as rationality, and intuition is a form of knowing analogous to observation.

There is, however, a longstanding hope in physics that, as one probes deeper and deeper into the theory, then the principles involved become steadily simpler. Then, as the universe unfolds, the idea is that more and more concrete details and complexity arises through "symmetry breaking", where the universe "makes choices" as to which path to take. So it is expected that there will be some sort of inchoate level. Some physicists, such as Roger Penrose, would in addition say that at this level one would not have to assume the principles of quantum theory as somehow given, but these principles themselves should emerge from the structure of the inchoate. While we do not have anything like this within physics at present, Parker-Rhodes gives us a unique vision of what it might be like.

So I shall be drawing not on the details of his work, but on the general picture which is endorsed in many other approaches. I shall illustrate these in the following diagram that superimposes the ouroboros of Chapter 6 onto the "Wheel" of Parker-Rhodes, combining metaphysical categories with the more conventional quantum mechanical ones.

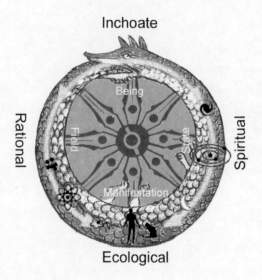

Inchoate

Rational

Spiritual

Ecological

The ouroboros of creation. From the origin, the inchoate, the point
where all opposites come together (the head and the tail) flow two
movements, expressed both in terms of aspects of being human (the
outer words) and in terms of quantum physics (the inner words and
the icons on the ouroboros).

In itself, prior to its unfolding in either physics or creation, the
inchoate is the silence that Eckhart pointed to, the fecund
nothingness that is disclosed when god rids us of God.

Two movements flow from the inchoate, two different directions of rotation of the wheel: one to the left towards the Platonic,
rational abstract structures of the quantum field; and one to the
right towards the actual overflowing of the One into created
reality. Though I have drawn them as if they stop when they meet
at the bottom, we need to think of them continuing through each
other, so that both are acting together at every scale of length. In
every context, spirit is calling existence out of matter, and each is
dependent on the other.

Looking first at the movement to the left of the diagram, on
the rational side, we can imagine the primitive logic of the

inchoate (in whatever form it might come to be known) as giving birth to successive waves of higher, more complex structure. Here, as in the whole of the flow in this direction, the dynamic is one of *emergence:* an ongoing repetition of the tension of a system that has many different potentials for growth, followed by the manifestation (evoked at any point where the two flows engage) of a new and hitherto unknowable form, creating a new context with new potentialities. In the very earliest stages there was no space or time and so we cannot think of this as an evolution in time; but there must have been some primitive germ of process, a seed for the cosmos.

In some such way as this, whatever were the first primitive forerunners of the quantum field began to begin to express themselves through the structures that were emerging, until, with the emergence of space-time, the quantum field could be expressed as something spread over space-time. Then further emergence, further taking on of being, enabled the dynamic of the field to segregate into the different forces we know now. Matter, Plato's *chora* or womb of becoming, repeatedly allowed the over-arching wholeness and meaning of the larger context, which is most often called spirit, to manifest new forms of being, and so allowed the emergence of new structures in the rational, field-like side of being.

In each context, emergence and creativity can be seen as two different ways of looking at the fundamental unfolding of being. Looking at it from the point of view of rational science, emergence is now a well-understood property of complex systems. From the point of view of quantum theory, both aspects are necessary for "being". The quantum field can do nothing without the quantum state. In particular, the quantum field defines how the quantum state changes in time and provides the context that interprets the quantum field. Yet even with both the field and the state together, manifestation — the emergence of actual existence, of one possibility rather than another —

remains mysterious when viewed only scientifically. The quantum state only captures the past. It defines probabilities for what might happen next, but it has no power to create the future. In quantum theory this creation of the future is constantly repeated, taking place at every moment, because (unlike classical theory) the present state does not determine the future unfolding of actuality[82]. For the full picture we need also to look at what is happening from the point of view of the intuitive, material side. Then what we see is creativity.

So if we follow this creative side, the movement to the right of the diagram, we can recall the stress that Eckhart laid when, in his Christian language, he described how we could find that we "worked one work" with God and thus shared in God's creativity. In more neutral language, we could say that, because the quantum state of each smaller context is inseparable from that of the larger context within which it is embedded, so the creative impetus of different structures of meaning flows from the greater context to the smaller. The creative drive echoes down from cosmos to galaxy to planet ... But in this direction of flow it is not just a matter of impassive physical influences. When this flow enters us, one of the medium-sized living organisms at the bottom of the circle, we feel the dynamic of action, of positive participatory engagement in the creative process.

This is the domain of religion, because its dynamic is the interplay of the creative overflowing of unity and the reaching out of love for a greater whole — love and unity being, as we have seen, the core of religion (though a core all too often obscured). Of course the word "love" only names the particular aspect that this creativity takes in human beings. But it does give us a particular perspective, one out of myriads, on the inner nature, the creative nature, of the emergence that science discerns throughout the universe. In the case of the human being we would name the active, participatory aspect of love as "free will"; but in other organisms scholars of complexity theory speak more cautiously of "agency" (from the Latin *agere*, to act). A bacterium, for example, can sense the direction in which food lies and may or may not *act*[83] and so initiates a new chain of cause and effect.

For manifestation, an intuitional language that talks about *meaning* is more appropriate that a propositional language that talks about causes. "Meaning", in the sense of power or "meaningfulness", is an expression of the richness of being with which an act or a thought is endowed. The more an act expresses the meaning of its immediate context, and the meaning of the greater contexts within which it is nested, the more likely it is that the act will bear fruit and make its mark on the world. So there is a chain of meaning cascading down from the inchoate into my particular acts. This is another way of speaking of the reaching-down of spirit (in the sense of pure being) into matter (the potential of the quantum state) so as to release a new form[84].

* * * * *** * * * *

This brings to an end my account of the "weaving" of the cosmos. The next two chapters will conclude this book by describing in more detail how this all works at the human level and drawing out its practical implications for action in today's world. But before this, there is one question I must address, though perhaps it is not one that has an answer at present:

> Is the universe really twofold, of rational and spiritual combined, or does it just appear that way because our human mind is twofold?

This is a particular version of the most central philosophical question, namely, how far is what we say we "know" a reflection of the world, and how far is it a reflection of our own minds/brains?

Our culture today rests under the shadow of two different ways of approaching this. The first is the scientific way. Science, it is claimed, has developed procedures for learning about the world which have been designed to extend to all suitably trained people in all cultures. There is no such thing as the Chinese scientific world-view or the African scientific world-view; there is only the (constantly developing and self-enriching) global scientific world view. On this view, the claim goes on, the world presents itself as if it had a real independent existence whose nature we were progressively unfolding through the scientific method of rigorously testing theories. Ultimately this is the only source of valid knowledge that we have.

The second way of approaching the question stems from that presented by the philosopher Emanuel Kant[85]. He like many philosophers in the later eighteenth century was concerned with the fact that we could never know the real nature of the world external to ourselves (as opposed to how it appears to us with our limited sense), or even be certain be certain that such a world exists. His solution involved two successive distinctions. First, he distinguished things as they appear to us from things as they are "in themselves", holding that, while there is only one world, we can only know it in relation to us and not in itself. Second, he divides the structure of the world as it appears to us into *manifestations*[86] (immediate sensory impressions of the world) and *a priori concepts*: that is, concepts like space and time which, he claims, are built into our nature prior to our observing anything, and which necessarily organise and shape our perceptions. He argued that these *a priori* human concepts were properties of our own thought, when thought was being properly applied, and were not properties of things in themselves. The latter were always, by definition, hidden from us. Kant's *a priori* concepts are called "transcendental", because they *go beyond* the properties of individual things and are inevitable aspects of the world as it appears.

These distinctions made by Kant might seem to increase our doubt and uncertainty about the world by making the nature of things in themselves completely mysterious. But because this nature was completely and permanently off-limits, it actually increased our certainty of the aspect of the world that we could know, and indeed provided a methodical programme for attaining that certainty, namely combining the careful experimentation of science for disclosing the appearances of particular things with the analyses of philosophy (we would add "psychology") for *a priori* concepts.

This programme seemed to be working well in Kant's own time, when science was still working close to our normal experience. Newtonian physics, for example, was based on Euclidean geometry, which Kant claimed to be able to show was a necessary *a priori* structure for any thinkable sort of space. Since then scientific theory has become abstract and its space has become curved, undermining Kant's neat distinctions, but I think that we can still learn from Kant's general approach. As human beings we map out a human sector in the realm of all possible ways in which the world can present itself. Indeed, we can think of each species of sentient being mapping out such a sector, with many overlaps. Our sector may not be static: our conceptual and perceptual equipment may change with time, growing in some areas and contracting in others. But it will always be the world as it appears to us, the world with which we are in relationship, that is the totality of the world as far as we are concerned, for the time being.

In Kantian terms, then, the twofold division of the world arises from the twofold nature of our sense-making apparatus. But if this duality is a transcendental property in Kant's sense, then it is an absolute and unavoidable aspect of the only world that we can know. The question, "is it the world or is it ourselves?" is a chicken-or-egg question.

The practical implication of this is that if we restrict our knowing to conventional rational science then we will be cutting down the "sector" of the human-knowable world even further, and by making this restriction, as modern Western culture does, we will inevitably be proceeding with blinkers on. By engaging our intuition as well (as we have been doing in this book) we can widen our account to a broader sector representing the full experience of mainstream human culture. It may be that aspects of mystical experience can extend this sector yet further, but that will be for others to judge.

In this spirit, I will move on to analyse in more detail this twofold nature of the human sector.

9

Humans

Latin Homo: from root in 'humus', Greek 'chamai' — on the earth.

In the last chapter we examined the universe on the largest possible scales of time and space, and saw how it was regulated by the two inter-flowing strands of rational (field) and intuitive/spiritual (state). Now we bring this insight home to the central question of what it is to be, and act as, human. Here, as I have stressed throughout, the same two strands are apparent.

For the philosophical reasons outlined in the last section of chapter 8, the substance of all existence appears to us as twofold, both at the cosmic and at the human level. It is thus to be predicted that the process of evolution (as we humans conceive it) has, through natural selection, developed ourselves as a species that responds to this duality. In particular, we have developed a twofold structure within ourselves: our rational and intuitive faculties. I will be describing this structure in some detail in this chapter, using one possible model for understanding it in terms of two separate organising mental subsystems. We will be seeing how these two subsystems weave their actions together in order to built the characteristic qualities of human behaviour and knowing.

We humans can not only think, but we can think about our thinking. And since our thinking is twofold, we can think about our thinking either rationally or intuitively. From the perspective of subjective, interior intuitive awareness, we call our thinking "mind", and from the perspective of external, rational examination we call it "brain". This opens up a delightfully complicating factor: we can think about our intuition intuitively or rationally, and we can think about our rationality intuitively or rationally! In this chapter, however, I will be describing our thinking mainly through rational analysis, with just a little poetic insight.

The twofold organisation of thinking is not a bare split, but (if it is to work at all) it includes a flow between its two poles. In terms of the structure of the universe as it appears to us this flow makes the universe also a unity, pervading everything. So, as I indicated at the end of the previous chapter, there is no warrant for those who wish to study the rational side of existence to claim exclusive authority. A purely "materialistic" (that is, rational) science will be self-consistent, but it can never be complete.

The answer to our starting question, of how we humans and the planet can flourish together now that we have control over the planet's destiny, now hinges on our learning to maintain the duality of our vision. Only then can we find our way back to the core of unity and love in our religious practices. Only then can we deploy our full creative abilities in responding to the needs of the planet. What will emerge from studying in this chapter a model of our own duality will be the idea that being human is all about "being-in-relationship": realising that my sense of "me" is made up from strong, substantial relationships with others, human and other than human, and from strong internal relationships within myself.

* * * * *** * * * *

To give substance to what I have just described, I now want to describe an example of a psychological description of the duality within ourselves. Whereas in physics it is often possibly to say, "this is the way it really is", psychological theories — in the present state of development of the discipline — are usually more cautious in their claims. Compared to my own discipline of physics, psychology is less developed because its subject matter, the human mind/brain, is far more complicated. Physics studies such things as simple atoms (a handful of particles moving round each other unperturbed by any neighbours), or the very early universe (before any confusing structures like galaxies appeared), or the properties of completely uniform and faultless crystal lattices; and on subjects like this physicists eventually reach agreement on theories that match the data, in so far as real objects match the physicists' idealisations. Psychologists, on the other hand, study the most complex system that we know, and in attempting to do this they have developed a wide variety of methods and types of theory. Each of these gives partial insight into aspects of human functioning, but there are fewer links than one would wish between one approach and another.

Psychological approaches vary in the sort of data they look at and their motivations (practical or theoretical) for doing so. They may consider introspection of thoughts (what I am aware of, from moment to moment); or verbal reports of this awareness; or behaviour; or the anatomy of the brain; or the functioning of the brain as revealed by a variety of scanning techniques. In all these cases psychologists can consider the effects of different sorts of interventions: magnetic fields, electrical brain stimulation, drugs, psychological therapies, meditation practices and so on. Increasingly, different modes are now being brought together, so that coherence across the discipline is growing.

Here I want to consider just one psychological theory out of the multitude available: the "Interacting Cognitive Subsystems" model[87] (ICS for short) developed by Philip Barnard and his collaborators at the Medical Research Council Cognition and Brain Sciences Unit at the University of Cambridge, UK. It has been developed to the point where it is very effective both in explaining the basic day to day behaviour and thoughts of human beings, and also in providing a framework for understanding what can go wrong with mental functioning and how to design psychological therapies to help people when this happens. It brings together many other less elaborate approaches that have been developed in clinical use[88], and so its general conclusions would be similar to these approaches.

The theory proposes that the brain works *as if* it consisted of a number of distinct units called "cognitive subsystems". This is regarded as a "model" rather than a literal description of the brain, in the sense that the brain does not necessarily contain specific anatomical structures or communication networks that correspond to all these subsystems (though this could be the case for some of the subsystems dealing with our senses[89]). It is, of course, highly simplified. The idea is to provide enough detail to cover a wide range of thought and behaviour, while keeping it simple enough for clinicians to use practically in understanding what is going on. Its importance for my argument here is that the two main subsystems of this model correspond to what I have been calling rationality and intuition. This will give us a much clearer idea of what these terms mean in practice.

The idea of something being made up of distinct units, each serving a different function, is familiar in the case of the machines we design, from TV sets to combine harvesters. A combine harvester, for example, turns growing wheat into grain, which requires a succession of processes — reaping, threshing, winnowing, sacking, baling — that need to be coordinated by a boss who is charge of the whole thing. So a combine harvester has a distinct physical section for each one of these processes and a central organiser, the driver, who coordinates the whole. One might think that the brain also had a similar series of distinct sections, with an overall boss-section that was "the real me". The surprising and important thing about the ICS model, however, is that THERE IS NO "BOSS" SUBSYSTEM. Instead there are *two* top-level meaning making subsystems that share the final control.

This means that I am behaving all the time as if I had the structure of a combine harvester driven by a two-headed eagle! In this model one of my top-level systems deals with the *implications* of what is going on in terms of my relationships with other people and objects in the world, their threats and opportunities. This is called the "implicational subsystem". The other top-level subsystem deals with understanding what is going on in a rational way, using logical propositions, and so it is called the "propositional subsystem". These are referred to for short as IMPLIC and PROP, respectively. The other subsystems (seven of them) deal with the senses, lower-level processing of sensory information and carrying out actions.

To get an idea of how this works, imagine that you are on safari and encounter a lion. Your eyes and ears will be picking up patterns of light and sounds. This information goes in two directions. One stream goes to systems which work out where the lion is, and from there to PROP, which then starts calculating whether you can get back in time to the truck you came in. The other stream goes from the senses straight to IMPLIC where it triggers a "Danger!" scheme of thought, and this in turn alters the state of your body into full alert, to react as fast as possible. Throughout this the two systems PROP and IMPLIC continually exchange information, coordinating the process. Together they constitute what Barnard calls the "central engine of cognition".

The following diagram shows how the information flows between these subsystems in this particular case.

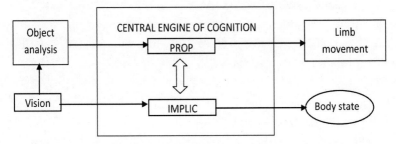

Just a few of the information routes (arrows) between some of the interacting cognitive subsystems (smaller rectangular boxes) of Teasdale and Barnard. "Body State" represents the effect of neural signals on the body: a separate subsystem (not shown here) feeds back the body state to the brain.

Most of our mental functions, or at least a representative set of them, are adequately described by 9 cognitive subsystems. We have just now met with 5 of them (the ones shown in rectangular boxes in the diagram above). "Body state" is not in itself a cognitive system; this label represents the processes that turn on the adrenaline and other hormones that switch the body into action. However it is closely linked with a further cognitive subsystem that monitors the body state and feeds the information back into the overall process. This subsystem has the same status as the sensory ones. The remaining three subsystems are: Hearing, Language processing (connecting words with sounds) and Speaking (making the sounds). Many other obvious systems (including the remaining senses) could certainly be added, but this would not introduce any new principles. All the subsystems work together in parallel, continuously exchanging information between them.

The diagram above illustrates two general principles about the differences between PROP (rationality) and IMPLIC ("intuition" in a very general sense)

- PROP has no *direct* input of data from the senses; but IMPLIC receives direct raw data from all the senses.
- The outputs of PROP go only to IMPLIC and to speech and limb movements, while the outputs of IMPLIC go only to PROP and to systems controlling the overall state of the body: our "gut reactions".

So, putting it very roughly, PROP is about understanding and doing, while IMPLIC is about feeling and reacting.

Most importantly, being human is not just about living in the immediate moment (though most of us could do with a lot more of that): it is also about memories. These not only underpin all our functions, but also contribute to our sense of self. The ICS model proposes that *each subsystem has its own memory records, where it stores information of the particular sort that is relevant to itself.* This is important when it comes to weighing up the evidence for ICS. For example, having separate memory records associated with IMPLIC and PROP explains why there can be such a big difference between "coolly" recalling, as in a novel, some past event, and having a "flashback" of just what a particular experience felt like. IMPLIC is closely connected with the senses, and so can easily reconstruct in a flashback the real feelings of the moment which are stored in the memories of the sensory systems; whereas PROP can only do this indirectly, via IMPLIC. This principle of separate memory stores also gives a very natural account of many phenomena of memory, such as why it is easier to remember words if their emotional "tone" (happy, sad, anxious etc) is similar to what one is actually feeling at the time. The data here are, however, complex and other theories can also explain this to some extent[90].

For the system to function at all it is absolutely essential for IMPLIC and PROP to work smoothly together, because separately they each have a seriously one-sided picture of what is going on. ICS tells us that it not just a matter of having both systems in action, giving both a rational and an intuitive perspective: they also have to be properly communicating with each other. For instance, PROP will always try to make a rational story out of what is happening, but if PROP gets out of touch with the other subsystems, this story can lose all touch with the reality of the situation. At a mild level this leads to clumsy and unhelpful actions, while at an extreme level the story gets detached from what is actually going on and thinking becomes psychotic. Building a flow between these two is the skill of Wisdom, which, as I proposed in chapter 2, was a characteristic of a healthy mediation between PROP and IMPLIC.

There are a few more technical provisions describing how information is shuttled around this system, whose details need not concern us here. The main point of these is that each subsystem has the same internal structure (a memory store and procedures and rules for moving information around) and all the subsystems are identical as far as this internal structure is concerned. They differ only with regard to how they are connected together and connected to other parts of the body, and with regard to the qualitative "meaning" of the information that they are receiving and storing, the subjective awareness we have when this information is being processed. As a result, the system is in its essence quite simple, but it is capable of producing enormously complex behaviours as a result of having (at least) 9 distinct components connected in distinct ways. The actual circuitry of neurons in the brain that underlies this will, of course, be infinitely more complex. But ICS carries the message that, first, the fundamental operations of the brain can, in broad terms, be explained comparatively simply; and, second, that there is no single "I" organising it. Instead, there is an experience that flows between all the subsystems, and there is a mental model of "me" (how I think of myself) that is largely centred round IMPLIC.

In the next section I want to explore how we get this sense of "me", and how the nature of this sense is crucial to the project of living in harmony with the earth.

* * * * *** * * * *

In chapter 1 we launched on a journey of discovering how we humans could behave so as to respect and care for the planet that we were now in charge of, and how we could stop behaving towards it like spoilt children. This is about relationship, our relationship with the planet, and for this relationship to be real and alive we need the understanding provided by our intuitive and rational sides. If we think of this in terms of society, then we need to engage (and reform with wisdom) the principle structures that feed these two sides of ourselves, namely religion and science. We also need to grasp how, as individuals, we need the smooth working together of these subsystems which enables us to act from the whole of our selves. When this is achieved, then we discover what it is to be truly human. Our life can flow in the way that our evolution has prepared us to live, in a way that is not destructive.

But "being human" sometimes seems difficult, compared to the life of other animals and birds. I've often gone outside on a spring morning and have been transfixed by the song of a blackbird perched on the topmost twig of the largest tree at the bottom of our garden; a song that flows out unstoppably with all the blackbird's energy and fervour. What grips me is not his energy, or a feeling of joy, or admiration of his skill ... it is the instinctive realisation in me that he is simply *being blackbird:* being, expressing, living what he is and overflowing with it.

The poet Gerald Manley Hopkins captured this in these lines from his poem, *As kingfishers catch fire, dragonflies draw flame:*

Each mortal thing does one thing and the same:
Deals out that being indoors each one dwells;
Selves —goes itself; myself it speaks and spells,
Crying Whát I do is me: for that I came.

It seems hard for us to be human in the same way that a blackbird is blackbird. We might be envious of the blackbird, who has only the IMPLIC to express and no PROP to confuse the issue. But now we know what the deal is, we can go forward. The issue is not, how do we avoid the split between rational and intuitive but, how do we work fully and freely with the split, with the propositional and implicational sides freely communicating and freely developing their own interpretations of what is going on? I think that the answer lies in that most important part of our lives: our significant relationships, whether with other people, with the earth and its life-forms, or with our own selves.

Relationships are closely bound up with the sense of "me": they shape that sense, and my model of "me" in turn shapes my subsequent relationships. My sense of "me", what sort of a person I am, where I stand in the world, is a collection of linked IMPLIC memory records[91] that is built up over our entire life. The clinical psychologist Isabel Clarke (yes, there is a connection!) has described how:

> "an individual's sense of self is constructed out of their experience of being in relationships from birth (and very probably before that in the womb) and throughout their subsequent experience. There is abundant evidence ... to suggest the fundamental role of the infant-caregiver dyad in the creation of meaning, communication and therefore a sense of self in the infant"[92].

Throughout the rest of our life this sense of self is shaped by a succession of relationships: and particularly by important and intimate relationships, with other people and also, as we shall be exploring in the next chapter, with places and landscapes that we grow to love. We *are* our relationships, in the sense that the "me" is built up of elements drawn from relationships. It is important to remember, however, that we are here dealing with IMPLIC memory, which stores overall feelings about the self and the world and is closely linked with the memories of sense-impressions. It is not about abstract concepts of the self (which are in PROP), but about the product of emotionally and sensorily "thick" chunks of actual encounters.

Along with my relationships with others who are important for me is what I might call "my relationship with myself". This is manifested in my overall reaction, in feelings and ideas, to this implicational "me" when I invoke it in the present moment. Does contacting the interior image of "me" make me feel contented, anxious, depressed, empowered ..? However others may have reacted to me in the past, how I react to "me" in any present moment can be altered. I can alter it myself by reflecting on whether my reactions are really valid, or by using a self-help system of affirmations, or, if I am seriously stuck, seeking professional psychological assistance. It is hard to have a good relationship with another person or a place if I have a negative feeling about one side of this relationship, namely myself.

The centrality of relationships, including my relationship with myself, takes us to the heart of why we are making such a mess of ourselves and of the planet. It is to do with the difficulty of facing pain: in particular, of facing the emotional pain of such things as knowing that we may be condemning our children and grandchildren to future suffering in a world racked by extreme global warming.

Processing pain, both physical and emotional, is one of the most important functions of IMPLIC. Physical pain tells us when our body is in danger and forces us to take care of it. A very few people are born with the inability to feel physical pain — a terribly dangerous condition because they are likely to carry on with their daily tasks after, say, breaking a limb and so inflicting great damage on their bodies. Similarly, feeling emotional pain is vital for the maintenance of our relationships. If we are separated from a loved one we feel emotional pain which drives us to be reunited with them, restoring our relationship. As individuals and as societies we have also evolved processes for healing emotional pain when a relationship is irreparably broken, as in bereavement where a process of mourning, assisted by the practices of one's community, gradually restores the fabric of the relationships that make up the self.

But what if our relationships are threatened by influences too vast and complex for us to deal with them through our instinctive reactions? This happens when we are trapped in an economic system that prevents us from finding a role in life, or when we are threatened by environmental change over which we feel we have no individual control. When it seems as though we cannot do anything about the imminence of severe emotional pain, the only strategy left to IMPLIC is to avoid ever thinking about it. And the best way of doing this is to constantly immerse yourself in an activity that gives you strong positive emotions. The result is addiction.

The theologian Matthew Fox (whom we meet again in the next chapter) has very clearly brought out the many different forms of this sort of addiction[93]. Of course, addiction to alcohol, drugs, self-harm, eating disorders and eating — all the obvious ones — are rife all around us. Fox added many of the seemingly harmless pastimes and lifestyle features of our society to the list of addictions: shopping, TV and cars, for instance. But these lifestyle addictions depend on the profligate use of energy and natural resources which is producing the horrible threat of climate change, which we are trying to avoid thinking about! We are trapped in a vicious circle, in which our avoidance of the painful emotions raised by climate change drives us to consume more and more, which make climate change worse.

I will examine this whole issue in detail in the next chapter. The vital point is that it is spirituality — the techniques of religion and the power of wisdom — which can break through this vicious circle. In practical terms it means turning to the care of our relationships with places and other than human creatures, care that comes from the growth of love for these beings, for love is the most basic relationship. Wisdom within spirituality engages the deliberate propositional side of our mind with the implicational side in breaking the circle of addiction. So in the light of this we can now understand in psychological terms why it is Pan, the god representing the natural world, who mediates between the intuitive (Eros) and the rational (Psyche).

* * * * *** * * * *

One of the main reasons why our relationships, with the earth, with humans and with ourselves, become thin or negative, is because the PROP subsystem becomes too dominant. PROP deals with the meaning structures of language, the faculty that is a distinctive capacity of human beings. Moreover, in the development of human culture over the millennia language has become more and more important. Look at what you and I are doing in writing and reading this book! So PROP becomes more and more dominant, and, as the centuries pass, our heads become more and more filled with the activity of PROP, with the "internal dialogue" that occupies most of the waking lives of those who make their living from language. So we tend to forget about the vital continuing role of IMPLIC — the subsystem that organises our relationships, builds our self, organises the storage of our deepest memories, generates our emotions and keeps constantly on the lookout for threats and opportunities. Ironically, we become unable to be our fully human selves because we over-emphasise the aspect of ourselves that makes us distinctively human.

When I am dominated by PROP, it is quite hard to take in, to savour the vibrant images and sounds that make up my total awareness. Instead of allowing these impressions, which reach me through IMPLIC, just to be themselves, I use PROP to turn them into words. For example, as soon as I turn my attention to a light patch glowing and vibrating on the wall, the words "sunlight … wall" waft into my mind, replacing the experience itself by words about the experience, a story about it. When the words always accompany the sensation, it can be hard to tell them apart. So I am always drifting away from the immediate reality of things and so prevented from truly relating to them.

The technique of mindfulness, associated with Buddhism, is helpful here. You learn to watch your own thoughts and experiences, letting them happen, not holding on to them, just quietly observing both images and words. It is common in mindfulness practice to use an image to assist this process. For instance I might use the background image of sitting on a river-bank watching the thoughts and experiences drift past as if they were boats. Often I find I have boarded one of the boats and I am being carried along with it, my internal dialogue chattering away. But on noting this I just disembark and continue watching.

After a while it becomes clear that images and words are different. It is like distinguishing the map from the territory: the map points to the territory but the map is not the territory.

In many activities — playing a sport, walking in a beautiful stretch of countryside — IMPLIC and the sensory subsystems take centre stage and PROP moves more into the background. Life becomes vibrant and rich, and I start to appreciate what is to be fully human. And in the course of this there may well be periods when I am open to aspects of my experience, usually my experience of the natural world, which are abundantly present but are not on the map of PROP. They overshadow the everyday furniture of life with a vividness and power that defies any description.

At first encounter these moments of the indescribable are all lumped together. They have the "numinous" quality that we have already identified, and which we can now identify as the characteristic quality of IMPLIC. Such experiences become the subject matter of religions, whose job it is to unite us with a greater world than that which can be fitted within language. At first we might say that we are "experiencing God". But most of the more developed religions can then lead one into a process of distinguishing the different varieties of such experience, and the richness of this other, intuitive part of our mind.

In our modern, technological and globalised world it is not enough, however, for all of us simply to open to both PROP and IMPLIC and to recognise the importance of the numinous The implicational subsystem is now the route whereby we can be manipulated by advertisers and politicians, whose images now replace the icons and pictures that we used to venerate in our churches. And our desire for the numinous can be filled by the drug dealers as well as by meditation. Alongside the two subsystems there needs to be wisdom: a learnt knowledge held within society and individuals which can discriminate between healthy and pathological practices. This was once the function of the religious traditions (who were often themselves guilty of perversely manipulating their members), but today it needs to be democratised to a more widespread knowing.

ICS gives a very coherent explanation of the "bilogic" of Matte Blanco which we encountered earlier. Translating this into the terminology of ICS, I suggest that IMPLIC behaves as if it had a symmetric logic, while PROP has an asymmetric logic. Asymmetric logic discriminates and separates, symmetric logic connects and amalgamates. Both these operations seem to be essential for creative thought. The group analyst Farhad Dalal[94] has argued that a mixture of symmetric and asymmetric logic is essential for language to operate. Concepts need to be brought together and identified with each other in order to form the classes underlying words, but then discrimination is needed to compile words into propositions. At this stage in the development of bilogic there seem to be strong parallels with the picture given by ICS, even though their premises are very different: the implicational subsystem, like symmetric logic, is concerned with highly compressed and interconnected general schemata regarding significance for the self; while the propositional subsystem, like asymmetric logic, is concerned with discrimination. They both flesh out, in rather different ways, the idea of the intuitive and the rational. While being aware that both these subsystems are only simple models of the vast complexity of the mind, I think it is still legitimate to align them in this way with Matte Blanco's two components of the logic of our minds, and regard them as complementary aspects of a basic division within our mind.

*   *   * * * * *** *   *   *

Earlier in this chapter I quoted part of a Hopkins poem praising how each mortal thing "selves", as a description of the basic essence of being, whether it is being a human or a blackbird. Following that we have seen how "me" is made up of two aspects, of which the implicational subsystem is the part that is concerned with the self, and the part we have in common with many other species, and so it seems that we need to attend to this part of our mind, to weave it well into our fabric, if we are truly to "selve". This subsystem is also the place of relationships, and so it seems, paradoxically, to be the case that we are most truly our selves when we are most deeply in our relationships.

We may recall from chapter 6 that Matte Blanco, as he explored the implications of symmetric logic at length, came to the conclusion that, as this component of bilogic increases, so we come closer to the religious experiences of the mystics. With this in mind I return to Hopkins, to inquire how he thinks that human beings selve. Here is the rest of the poem following the quotation, giving Hopkins' own answer to this question:

> Í say móre: the just man justices;
> Kéeps gráce: thát keeps all his goings graces;
> Acts in God's eye what in God's eye he is —
> Chríst — for Christ plays in ten thousand places,
> Lovely in limbs, and lovely in eyes not his
> To the Father through the features of men's faces.

So Hopkins' answer is a religious one, and thus for him a Christian one — though a similar answer could be made from the perspective of many other religions. In concrete though challenging terms, being human is "justicing" and "keeping grace". In more religious and more global terms, it is, for him, expressing that universal essence of humanness that Christians believe was embodied in Jesus.

10

Ecology

From Greek: oikos — house, dwelling + German logie (Greek: logos) — area of knowledge

Our starting point in this book was the realisation that humanity was in crisis; that our current behaviour makes it impossible for us to live in peace with each other and with the environment; that we are behaving like children given the run of a toy store. We then saw how being human involves the balanced working together of our intuition and our reason (the implicational and propositional subsystems) and how our failure to live peacefully was due to our failure to understand our own twofold nature and bring it into balance. Achieving a wise harmony in ourselves, in our society and in the planet all went together. In this final chapter I will spell out in more detail how the crisis of climate change is even now providing the stimulus and the opportunity for humanity to achieve this change; how we can turn our immense ingenuity and capacity for organisation towards good rather than ill, and how this is already happening.

To achieve increasing harmony is society we will need the links between science and religion that I have been developing in past chapters, and which I will take forward in this chapter. Ecology will play a central role in this, in more ways than one. Its ideas can extend both into science and into spirituality; and in addition ecology can be a "place" where we can encounter nature and where we can judge how wisely we are integrating our intuitive and rational sides by seeing the effect that we have on nature. Nature provides in this way a concrete experienced reference point to which we can relate our thoughts and actions. The result of enlarging our own self to embrace nature in this way has been called "the ecological self". I will describe this concept, which is destined to play a major role in the growth of human knowing, in more detail here.

The reuniting of science and religion entails a significant change in religion, back to its core values of unity and love, now seen in an ecological context. I will describe how this change is happening through the major faiths and in the growth of new religious movements. This change in religion involves particularly a change in religious *practice* (what one actually does in ones religion), which I will illustrate from my own experience.

* * * * *** * * * *

I will begin with climate change. This is the driver for a change in society. Only climate change can arouse an urgency to unite the world in a common enterprise. The political status of climate change has altered dramatically over the last two years. In March 2007 it was possible for the UK television "Channel 4" to broadcast a programme called *The Great Global Warming Swindle* using long discredited ideas as "evidence" to claim that that the current level of carbon emissions did not pose any threat to the planet. Moreover, when the programme was reviewed by the official television regulator "Ofcom", the makers were found guilty only of a technical irregularity. Now, two years later, a programme like this would, to most informed people, seem as offensive as a programme denying the holocaust or advocating free handouts of heroin to children.

It took a long time for public and political opinion to get to this point, however. The main action started in 1988 when the United Nations set up a body of scientists from a wide range of countries — the Intergovernmental Panel on Climate Change or IPCC — to evaluate the risk of climate change caused by human activity. At that time the "greenhouse effect", the idea that gases in the earth's atmosphere could trap the heat of the sun and thereby increase the temperature, was well known among scientists, but there was a lot of uncertainty about its details, and it was not even clear whether human activity would increase or decrease the effect. In 1990 the panel reported that "Based on current models, we predict: under [the 'business as usual' scenario] increase of global mean temperature during the [21st] century of about 0.3°C per decade (with an uncertainty range of 0.2 to 0.5°C per decade); this is greater than that seen over the past 10,000 years; under other ... scenarios which assume progressively increasing levels of controls, rates of increase in global mean temperature of about 0.2°C [to] about 0.1°C per decade." They went on both to outline the dangers from sea level rises that this warming would cause and also to draw attention to the significant uncertainties in these predictions at the time of writing.

In 1995 the panel produced a second report in which they cited clear evidence, from past correspondences between human carbon emissions and variations in climate, that human activity did have an influence on the climate, stating that: "the probability is very low that these correspondences could occur by chance as a result of natural internal variability only." By this stage they had reached a good understanding of the physical mechanisms involved in climate change, from which it was clear that what humans did would alter the future temperature, and that changes in what we did were necessary in order to stop serious damage in the 21st century.

The process for producing the periodic reports of the IPCC, which has representatives from over 100 countries, is for the scientists to analyse all the research in three working groups which report separately in detail on what has been learned. In 1995 these reports totalled 1898 pages. After this, three "Summaries for Policy makers" are produced. It is these summaries that will be read by government advisors, and a consensus is required from every one of the countries making up the panel. By December 1995 this summary process was deadlocked, with two countries, Saudi Arabia and Kuwait, refusing to accept the drafts. Mohammad Al-Sabbar, a Saudi ministerial adviser, declared that: "Until there is clearer evidence of human involvement in climate change we will not agree to what amounts to a tax on oil."[95] By mid December the summaries had been released with many key clauses deleted, including a call for "strong policy measures", a list of "policies and instruments" that were needed, and the warning that the timescale for action was "a few decades"[96]. It was also reported that the USA had not been helpful in this process.

Imagine being in a bus being driven fast towards what appears to be a brick wall. Several passengers get out binoculars and confirm that it does indeed look very like a brick wall, causing a certain amount of concern among those in the front of the bus. But two passengers with a taste for speed are enjoying the ride. They call out loudly that there is no real evidence that it is a brick wall and that everything is OK, while urging the driver to accelerate onwards. The passengers are reassured, they settle down in their seats, and the driver is happy to oblige and put his foot down. Such, almost unbelievably, was the situation with the bus of international politics from 1995, through the IPCC's third report in 2001, up to their fourth report in 2007.

The trouble is that what drives human beings to make tough decisions is the intuitive subsystem, IMPLIC. And the logic of this subsystem doesn't deal with past and future. Time does not exist here, as we can learn from all those sources which we have examined in previous chapters: Matte Blanco, the mystics and the psychologists. There is nothing intermediate between now and eternity. Nor does IMPLIC deal with nuances of probabilities. Time and probabilities are the domain of the rational subsystem PROP.

In the plenaries of the IPCC in 1995 things were getting tough and IMPLIC had the bit between its teeth.

"Will I get oil to run all our cars and planes now?" it cries.

"Yes", is the reply.

"Will I always get it?"

"Some people say no."

"Then shut them up."

With each passing year the science became clearer. Soon it was possible to work out in reliable detail exactly how climate responded to different scenarios for human activity. Importantly, the methods used were robust against any variations in the small details of the process that were still not pinned down. Whatever one assumed about these details, the same large-scale results were obtained[97]. But now it was not a matter of a 1-degree temperature rise: the predictions were now talking about a rise of from 4 to 6 degrees by the end of the 21st century. The human and political consequences of this, which were spelled out in detail, were almost unimaginable: the major parts of many countries submerged under the sea; many countries that are now prosperous exporters of food consigned to mass starvation. And in the months since 2007, it transpired that many effects had still been under-estimated. In particular, the polar icecaps were seen to be melting much faster than had been predicted.

"The Great Global Warming Swindle" television programme simply ignored all this, and presented arguments that had been completely refuted in the 1980s, so as to produce a façade of rationality. It was the clearest possible example of an attempt to manipulate the population by skilfully playing on their implicational side and duping their propositional side. The illusion only lasted a few months, however. There was now no watering down of the IPCC summaries, and the truth soon hit home. The situation was, and is now critical after the twelve wasted years since global warming was demonstrated in 1985. But in the last two years governments have started lumbering into reluctant action.

*   *   *   * ****   *   *   *

Climate change has roused us out of our mental sleep in which we have ignored the effect that we humans have on the earth. The issue is now widely regarded as serious, and there is a gradually increasing realisation that there is a need for a global mobilisation of our technical and intellectual resources to combat the threat that is posed to humanity. I applaud this and try to play my part.

But while this is all completely true, I want to take the discussion further than this. I want to argue that climate change is not only a threat, but also an opportunity. We are now awake! And being awake we are also able to tackle many other problems which, not surprisingly, seemed too difficult when we were asleep. We have awoken to thinking of the earth as a whole, with ourselves living in it and affecting it as a whole as we interact and relate to the great web of species other than us humans living on this planet. As I have described here, relationships are what our human selves are made of, and so we are all being drawn into a greater sense of our selves as extending out into this web of species. I suggest that because of this the way is opening for us to discover the wisdom needed for reconnecting the rational and intuitive strands in individuals and in society. We have the opportunity not just of tackling climate change, but becoming able to live fully human lives.

Awareness of the web of species is the fundamental principle of the science of ecology, and so I now turn to that. The word "oecologie" (translated into the English "ecology") was first coined in 1866 by the German naturalist and evolutionary biologist Ernst Haeckel, to describe the study of total systems of organisms together with their environment. Some years later a British writer explained that "[Ecology] chiefly rests on the exploration of the endless varied phenomena of animal and plant life as they manifest themselves under natural conditions". Then from the 1950s the idea of systems and environments became more generalised and spawned a succession of "eco" words — ecocultural, ecohistorical, ecopsychological and so on — and from the 1970s the word was also used with a focus on how human beings affected natural environments, usually for the worse[98]. As the significance of climate change struck home, so "ecology" extended its meaning to refer to all aspects of the way organisms interact together to fashion life on our planet. It included the theoretical science of these interactions, their practical implications, their emotional impact on how we live, the factors that affect how we engage with the environment, and so on.

The basic context within which we humans exist, whether we realise it or not, is the planetary ecosystem — that is to say, the planet considered as a system of organisms within their environments. We saw in chapter 8 that there was a very real sense in which the entire cosmos is our ultimate context, spiritually speaking; but its influence is felt at a deep level and for most of the time we need something more tangible. For the majority of us in the developed world, the context that we are most aware of is that of our workplace, our home and immediate family. But though very tangible, this is too restricted a context. It can blinker us to the vital relations we have with the wider world. The planetary ecosystem lies in between these two. It is not so wide and deep that we cannot grasp it, nor so limited that it is inadequate. It is our true "oikos" or home, a living home with which we have living relationships.

*   *   * * *** *   *   *

Most importantly, ecology has the capacity to bring together science and religion and to heal the rift between them. This, more than anything else, can liberate humanity into a lasting ecological consciousness. In earlier chapters I have described how the processes of science and religion are intertwined, and in particular how the concept — or rather, experience — of Being is pivotal for both science and religion. Yet despite the abundant correspondences between the two which I have drawn out I cannot yet point to real changes in the rift that are happening here and now. The problem is that science and religion have grown so far apart, both as regards their implicational aspects (stronger in religion) and their propositional aspects (stronger in science), that one can hardly imagine at present what a genuine mutual linking of the two would be like.

Research so far towards uniting science and religion has been fascinating and inspiring, but still seems like a mixture of analogies between science and religion rather than an organic working together. An important example is the work of Allan Wallace, who is highly qualified by his training in both Tibetan Buddhism and in science, the former being very extensive. He has suggested[99] that the different states of the vacuum that cosmologists believe are involved in the very earliest stages of the universe correspond to certain different awarenesses of consciousness at the deepest levels of meditation. It is a fascinating suggestion, but there are problems. The contexts of the two situations are wildly different. Moreover the cosmological situation depends on a particular mathematical form for the laws governing the fields present at that stage, while the meditative experience is one of the absence of any form. The link, which may be only a loose analogy, does not seem to shed any light on the most fundamental stage of symmetry breaking, namely the emergence, in the apparent absence of any external observer, of the "fluctuations" that give rise to the galaxies and stars which we examined in Chapter 8.

To take another example, Roger Penrose and Stuart Hameroff[100], Henry Stapp[101], and myself[102] have produced related but independent accounts of quantum theory which have a place for consciousness. Consciousness, with its role as the essence of being that stands as a complement to form (as described in the chapter 8) opens up a link with spirituality and so can be an important link between science and religion. But the snag is that in all of these papers it is not clear why it should be consciousness, rather than just some particular sort of physical field, that enters into the processes of neurons in the brain.

*   *   * * **** *   *   *   *

In both the examples I have just described, of the vacuum states of the universe and of consciousness, the problem is that as scientists we have inadequate skill in moving backwards and forwards between the implicational and propositional ways of knowing, and as a result we get stuck in the propositional, losing the essential intuitive insight of the implicational.

In the universe, as we saw in the last chapter, the quantum state becomes manifest in a concrete way, and then evolves further under the influence of the quantum field, so that the processes of the universe seemingly move backwards and forwards between the realisation of being and the creation of form. This alternation might give a clue to how we can engage with the universe through both our intuitive and rational sides. To avoid getting trapped in the rational it is best to describe this mythically, using ideas introduced into Christianity by the pioneer of eco-spirituality, Matthew Fox (whom we met briefly in the last chapter). He recalls the figure of Wisdom (hokma) in the Bible who was present with God in the act of creation:

> The LORD brought me [Wisdom] forth as the first of his works,
> > before his deeds of old;
> I was appointed from eternity,
> > from the beginning, before the world began.
> Then I was the craftsman at his side.
> > I was filled with delight day after day,

rejoicing always in his presence,
rejoicing in his whole world
and delighting in mankind[103].

This gives us the picture of a dance between God and Wisdom, weaving backwards and forwards as first one then the other leads, delighting in each other. From this dance there spins out, like sparks from a Catherine wheel, intertwining waves of being and meaning[104]. This dance links the themes of this book with the Judaic tradition, when we interpret Being and Meaning with both our intellect and our intuition.

If we discover something, such as seeing the Milky Way on a dark night, or encountering the smell of elderflower on a spring morning, that discovery involves both the being of thing (it's there!) and its meaning for us ("it's a ..."). For it to register with us at all, we need to have categories of meaning with which to grasp it. To give an example, in most parts of the UK the background light from towns at night makes it impossible to see any but the brightest stars and planets, so that many people here have never seen the milky way. I have on more than one occasion, when staying with a group in one of the few places where the sky is not polluted by street lights, asked someone, as they return from looking at the sky at night, "did you see the milky way?" and they have answered, "no." And when I pursued the question and described it, they still affirmed that they had not seen it. But when we went out together, and I pointed it out, it was thereafter seen as the most wonderful part of the whole sky. If we are presented with a perception that we cannot classify there is a moment of confusion, even of mild distress, as we struggle to pigeonhole it, to make it a "thing" rather than a don't-know-what.

The Bible chapter from which the quotation above comes is in fact mainly taken up with naming things: "When there were no oceans, I was given birth, when there were no springs abounding with water; before the mountains were settled in place, before the hills, I was given birth, before he made the earth or its fields or any of the dust of the world. I was there when he set the heavens in place, when he marked out the horizon on the face of the deep, when he established the clouds above and fixed securely the fountains of the deep..." We find the same cataloguing of instances, of the meanings of things as expressed by names, in the last chapters of the book of Job, when God reveals his nature as Creator, and in the Bhagavad Gita where Krishna discloses a similar revelation to Arjuna. Creation, in these myths, wasn't just the production of 'stuff'; it was about the production of this, and that, and those ... It was a meaningful universe, as well as a manifestation of being.

In the example of the milky way we seem to be talking about perception, about how we need to supply a label in order to perceive what is there whether we know it or not. What was shocking about quantum theory was the discovery that, because the possibilities for existence were logically incompatible (the complementarity principle), some meaning, in the form of a context, had to be supplied before anything could come into being. Meaning was supplied as one of the array of particular windows on reality that collapse the fluid logic of the inchoate to the Aristotelian logic of the classical world. At first some physicists linked this with the idea of our supplying meaning when we make an act of perception, and supposed that it was the perception of the physicist that was supplying meaning, just as we supply meaning when we struggle to make sense of an unfamiliar perception. But soon, as I have described, it was realised that the universe itself could supply meaning; the universe was imbued with meaning.

This is to look at meaning through the eye of reason. But when we look on meaning through the eye of intuition instead, we see meaning as something more. We can be struck by "meaningful coincidences". This is the realm of the implicational, the system that can flag up things that need our attention by endowing them a feeling of significance, If uncontrolled by the propositional it can result in everything been suffused in this "meaning feeling", which is both exciting and disorientating. Just as meaning as context turned out to be something that flowed through the universe as a whole, so it could be that meaning as significance is also something greater than the human, playing a role in which of the possibilities that are allowed in quantum theory actually manifests on a particular occasion and in a particular context. The words of Wisdom just quoted evoke this sense of meaning as an intangible significance, which asserts the perfect rightness of that which is being born from eternity into the lightness of Now. Embracing Wisdom, as the go-between linking intuitive and rational, involves allowing ourselves to feel and recognise this rightness in our daily acts.

There is also more to Being. It also has two aspects according to which part of our mind in prevailing. With the eye of reason, and the context of Newtonian physics we see Being as matter, in the sense of the stuff of existence that requires a form (meaning) to become a particular "this". In the context of quantum physics, where there is no such thing as matter in this sense, being is the quantum state which rolls forward the weight of history, presenting the Now with the factual constraints coming from the past, with their particular possibilities – the concrete embodiment of what is the case, out of which can manifest the next particular creation.

With the eye of intuition, however, we see being after this act of creation that occurs anew in every moment. Then we encounter a whole thing, the stars of the milky way, the smell of the blossom, the mystery of a living creature, encountering it not as an abstraction but in relationship, as "Thou", the beloved who, in Buber's words "fills the heavens" with his/her pure existence, who silences separation in a shower of love.

*   *   * * *** *   *   *   *

While it may be in fundamental physics that a re-uniting of these ways of knowing may produce the most far reaching changes in both science and religion, I am convinced that it is in the realm of ecology that this breakthrough can happen soon; which is fortunate since it is precisely here that we urgently need some new and inspiring thinking.

It seems to be in the nature of ecology that it can rarely be confined to an academic science, but overflows into a spiritual relationship. I have never come across any naturalist or ecologist who does not have a love and wonder for the creatures and landscapes that they investigate, whether or not they express it, whether or not they allow it come into their professional work. The mere fact of being outside and paying attention draws you into a relationship with the terrain around you. And if your scientific brief is to pay attention to the way the different organisms are linked to each other, perhaps with a view to maintaining these linkages, then your relationship will be one of unity, and thereby of love — in the sense I defined earlier of "the extension of oneself, usually for the benefit of another." Darwin's writings, for example, are filled with wonder and amazement at what he is discovering; as well as perplexity, because it did not fit with the external form of religion as he had known it.

An ecological approach is already producing works where we see the author genuinely grasping both the implicational and propositional ways of knowing. Freya Mathews' book *For Love of Matter* (which strongly influences this book) is mainly about the personal spiritual significance of the nature of matter, while being interpenetrated with the insights of her earlier book *The ecological self*, a concept I will examine shortly. She links this concept with physics, particularly General Relativity. Similarly, Stuart Kaufman's recent book *Reinventing the Sacred* keeps the intuitive meanings of "sacred", "agency", "life" and so on firmly in mind, while re-expressing them in terms of a general mathematical approach to ecology and evolution.

Ecology takes us on to the issue of "Gaia", another area where reason and intuition can combine. James Lovelock, a scientist, inventor and visionary, famously claimed, as a result of his research on the atmosphere, that the planetary ecosystem was itself a living organism, which he named Gaia after the Greek word for "earth". Gaia was regarded as a goddess by the Greeks, but Lovelock did not go so far. When he claimed the earth was a living organism he meant, I believe, that it was a system that could maintain its diverse, complex structure while poised in space within the dynamic environment of the stream of energy from the sun, whose strength waxes and wanes over timescales from years to millions of years. This ability to flourish amidst, indeed because of, a changing environment, is often regarded as the essence of a living being.

As a physicist I like to look at this from the point of view of different sorts of equilibrium (this is part of the science of thermodynamics). Strictly speaking, in physics the word "equilibrium" means a state when nothing is moving or changing. If you put a cube of ice into a vacuum flask full of hot water, at first there is change as the ice melts, but eventually the system reaches equilibrium in which everything is the same temperature and nothing is changing. Equilibrium is very boring. Slightly more interesting is what might be called dynamic equilibrium. If I prop up a stone in front of a hot fire, after a while a steady state will be reached in which one side of the stone is hot and the other cool, with a steady flow of heat travelling through it. There is still nothing really happening, but at least the flow of energy is a dynamic movement.

Each planet in our solar system is suspended in the flow of energy from the sun like a stone in front of a fire. Unlike the stone, most of the planets are rotating and have atmospheres. As a result, many of them have weather: visible swirling storms.

This gets more interesting. Something quite complex is going on. But I would hesitate to say that weather is in itself "life" or constitutes an "organism". We come to know the life that flows within Gaia gradually, from the inside, as we start to form relationships with its living parts, and as we come to understand in wonder the intricacy of relations between them. We acknowledge that it is indeed an indivisible whole when we meditate on the famous NASA photograph of the earth hanging in space, immersed in the flow of heat from the sun, not passively transmitting this heat and light to the surrounding darkness of space, but using every speck of it to nurture its own structures as this energy filters through the web of living creatures.

Our need is not to get outside of Gaia, like the astronauts, valuable as their experience has been. It is to get inside of Gaia, to immerse ourselves more deeply in our relationship with the expanding circles of life that we find around us.

*　　*　　*　*　***　*　　*　　*　　*

The enlarged self that we can now find as we grow within Gaia, the self with the wisdom to navigate the flow between rational and intuitive, has been called the *ecological self*. The name was first introduced by Arne Naess in 1985. Later he defined it as "that with which [a person] identifies", where by "identifies" he understands "a spontaneous, non-rational . . . process through which the interest or interests of another being are reacted to as our own." The idea is rooted in his own experience. He describes how:

"I looked through an old fashioned microscope at the dramatic meeting of two drops of different chemicals. A flea jumped from a lemming strolling along the table and landed in the middle of the acid chemicals. To save it was impossible.

It took many minutes for the flea to die. Its movements were dreadfully expressive. What I felt was, naturally, a painful compassion and empathy. But the empathy was not basic. What was basic was the process of identification, that 'I see myself in the flea'. If I was alienated from the flea, not seeing anything resembling myself, the death struggle would have left me indifferent."[105]

The ecopsychologist Elizabeth Ann Bragg sums up the concept of ecological self in the following points:

(1) Ecological self is a wide, expansive or field-like sense of self, which ultimately includes all life-forms, ecosystems and the Earth itself.
(2) Experiences of ecological self involve:
(a) an emotional resonance with other life-forms;
(b) a perception of being similar, related to, or identical with other life-forms;
(c) spontaneously behaving towards the ecosphere as one would towards one's small self (with nurture and defence).
(3) It is possible to expand one's sense of self from the personal to the ecological.[106]

We can now start to understand how the ecological self can provide the wisdom needed to restore a right balance between our implicational and propositional systems. The problem that we face in our society is that these systems all too easily collude with each other to produce behaviour that is destructive to ourselves individually and to our environment. Most of us in the West live in built environments that are hard to relate to, with our days organised to suit commercial pressures rather than our human needs, and our human interactions concerned with control or compliance rather than with love and creativity. As a result, our implicational system – on the lookout for potential threats to our well-being – is constantly on edge. The way out is for the propositional subsystem to concoct a story, a self-image of "me", that is as reassuring as possible. It tells me, for instance, that my way of life is the best possible one because I have lots of possessions and that the problems arise from malevolent groups bent on attacking my affluent way of life. The title "Global Warming Swindle" that I quote earlier epitomises this. It weaves a story that everything is really OK and the problem lies with a bunch of perverse Greenies who are out to fool us. The implicational subsystem responds to this by feeling happy when in front of the television set and fearful when encountering Greenies, thus reinforcing the propositional story by proving that affluence is good and Greenies are bad. The two subsystems lock each other into a destructive cycle.

The way out of such cycles is to introduce a third point of reference, and if possible to incorporate this reference point as a source of wisdom in oneself. We might find this in the people around us, but if we are in a society where everyone is telling the same story this is often impossible. The reference point of Gaia stands right outside these destructive stories. When I am in my ecological self, the trees and the plants around me assure me, by their beauty and fragility, that they are what makes life worth living, but that all is in fact not well and a change is required that will both bring me into contact with the joy of knowing their beauty and will also preserve them for the future.

Knowledge of ecology is the scientific key to building a sustainable world. But more than this, a realisation of the wonder of ecology is likely to lead to a real relationship within the web of life, and this is likely to lead to a growth of the ecological self, which brings the wisdom to allow our intuitive and rational sides to work together positively instead of negatively. This is why ecology is so crucial to the state of humanity today.

* * * * *** * * * *

There are also grounds for hope in religion, as well as in ecology, and I will describe some of these in more detail shortly. We have seen that the traditional religious faiths hold at their core the principles of love and unity that can transform humanity and humanity's relation to the planet. But in many places and times these faiths have in reality been agents for dogmatism: they have clung to the opposite of these principles, through a failure to direct the power of the intuitive by integrating it with the rational. Some Islamic societies, for example, have pretended that tribal practices that oppressed women were compatible with Islamic law[107]; the Roman Catholic Church has used mediaeval Aristotelian philosophy to obstruct the control of population through the use of contraceptives; the American Protestant church has used a perversely narrow approach to the Bible in order to subvert the teaching of evolution within science; and many religious traditions in India have held in place a widespread network of superstitions that hold back adequate medical treatments. All these abuses of religion have been well charted, by atheist writers, in particular. The forces of genuine religion and quasi-religion have for many centuries seemed balanced. For every Torquemada torturing "heretics" in the inquisition there has been, on the other side of the balance, a Wilberforce abolishing slavery.

As society tends to become more aware of the dangers of superstition and of disguising tribal violence as religion, one would expect that religion would move back to its roots in love, justice, unity and compassion. In recent years, however, this has not been so. The reactionary wings of religion have shown few signs of withering away. Where religion could be coming to the aid of our human problems, it is instead retreating into dogmatism, and hence antagonising those who do not identify with any faith tradition. Atheists such as Richard Dawkins, who see only the dogmatism, have responded by an understandable public attack on religion, and this has in turn strengthened the feeling of the dogmatists that they are engaged in some kind of all-out war between God and Satan.

It is not hard to see how this tragic state of affairs is being driven by our failure to appreciate our two ways of knowing and use wisdom to integrate them. Once sacred texts were responded to in a way that integrated the intuitive and the rational: the literal meaning was present, but it was modulated and interpreted by symbolic meanings that flow from the intuitive. This is the true meaning of "myth". It does not just mean something that is not true, it means something that derives a deeper truth from its double meaning. Now, however, dogmatists in religion take the passion and certainty that they derive from the intuitive (the implicational) and apply it blindly to a literal reading of the text, producing a perversion of the tradition. The atheist scientists, on their side, rightly stress the importance of rational science, but are blind to the importance of the intuitive in religion, and sometimes (not, however, in the case of Dawkins) blind to the role of the intuitive in their own work.

At several times in earlier centuries Islam and Christianity were in the vanguard of scientific discovery and in the vanguard of exhibiting the integrating power of Wisdom. This knowledge has continued more consistently in the Eastern faiths and in the primal religions of the indigenous peoples, but the majority of scientists have been so concerned with focussing their hostility on the Abrahamic religions that the contributions of these other faiths have to often gone unnoticed. It is time now for the liberal wings of all the faiths to return to their traditional position of wisely combining our ways of knowing, and allow those who confuse spiritual tradition with tribal dogmatism to simply become irrelevant.

In fact, things are now changing in many ways. Hope within religion lies in a growing diversification. Within each faith more communities and congregations are finding the confidence to stand for justice and peace, both in faiths like Roman Catholicism, which strives to cling to a monolithic uniformity, and in faiths like Islam where individual mosques have always been autonomous. In addition, many "new religious movements" are springing up, finding their own inspiration in different practices and different writings.

In such a diverse situation, the touchstone for what is true and valid lies not in adherence to formal creeds, but in the effectiveness with which a religious grouping promotes justice for people and for the planet: in the way it responds in respect and love to the whole natural order. In the future it will become increasingly the case that religions are not classified by the particular traditions of Islam, Buddhism etc. but by whether or not they preach a narrow tribal dogmatism or a full revelation of universal justice. In a tribal reading of their traditions the implicational side is locked into a state of fear and the propositional is recruited into supporting this; while in a teaching of justice the implicational expands in love and the propositional is used to discriminate between true universality and mere emotionalism. An effective response to this challenge of discrimination requires, and encourages, a right working together of the propositional and the implicational. And above all, it is in the realm of ecology that a mediation between these two faculties can and should be developed.

Giving attention to our implicational side, to counterbalance the propositional, draws attention to the importance of *practices* in religion: regular exercises designed to expand the mind (or, in the terminology of some religions, the "spirit") and thereby learn to know and act more faithfully. In particular, we can inquire into the extent to which religious practices can engage with ecology and thereby enable our integration with the planet at the same time as they enable our inner integration.

One factor in considering religious practices is that

Christianity often lags behind other religions. In my late teens I dabbled in Buddhism, before deciding (perhaps simplistically) that all major religions had a universal content, differing only in their form, in a way analogous to the way in which different map-projections execute different images of the world. Consequently, I felt that I would lose nothing essential, and gain in convenience, by adopting the religion of my own culture, and I switched to Christianity. After the conversion experience that I described in Chapter 1 I turned up at the church in my home town and asked the curate there what Christians did, corresponding to the meditation practices of Buddhism. He seemed thoroughly confused by the question and waved me towards a small shelf of books for sale, in the hope that they might be useful (which they weren't).

This situation is now changing. Were I to ask the same question now, I could be directed to texts on practices analogous to meditation, such as the ancient Greek Orthodox practice of repeating, in time with the breath, the short "Jesus prayer", or the forms of Christian mantra meditation developed by Lawrence Freeman, or Thomas Keating's "centering". Or I might be directed to more distinctively Christian practices that integrate the propositional and the implicational, such as the Augustinian and Benedictine practice of "Lectio Divina" in which a passage of scripture is mentally perused very slowly through a series of stages so as allow the words to sink down into the unconscious.

* * * * *** * * * *

This picture, which could also be drawn within most of the major religions, points to a recovery of the integrative practices that we need in order to develop a wise discernment between religion's living core of love and unity, and the outward dead shell of dogmatism.

Many people have a much more developed and natural ecological self than I: nonetheless, it may be helpful to enlarge on the events, mentioned earlier, which have nurtured my ecological self. For me, expanding from the personal to the ecological has on many occasions brought me nuggets of wisdom and understanding; not only about my relations with Gaia, but also about personal issues.

I first met this at a workshop where the leader described a process of finding a tree and asking it questions. The procedure was as follows. You would walk out into the countryside, wandering with the intent of being drawn to some particular tree. When this happened you would sit underneath it, facing each of the four compass directions in turn. In each direction you would "ask the tree" a question and wait for an answer. The questions were prescribed in advance, such as "who am I?" or "where am I going?".

At the time I had felt a strong need to understand what my direction in life would be, and so I gave this a try. I set off in what I think of as a spirit of pilgrimage, a spirit of being led along a sacred path whose exact goal you do not know, but where you are holding a firm intention of following where you are led. I passed many trees without feeling any particular attraction, and eventually found myself in a patch of woodland that I did not know, where I was drawn off the track towards an old tree with low hanging branches. There I sat facing East, mentally enunciated the first question and waited.

It was probably an hour or so before anything happened. In my case, it usually takes time for me to shift gear into the sort of empty mind where I am no longer listening to my inner chatter, but am open to the arrival of something new. An answer came in the form of a verbal thought, accompanied by an "aha!" of recognition, that this was indeed new information. The subsequent questions flowed rather more rapidly.

I would not say either that I specifically "asked the tree" or that it was the tree that "answered". Rather, the tree was a presiding presence for the whole operation. This is where the idea of the ecological self comes in. The tree was the immediate specific representative of the larger web of life, and sitting under the tree, coming into relationship with the tree, enabled me to extend my self to this wider context. Standing in the wider context, it no longer was helpful to ask whether the "answer" came from within me or from something greater. I would say that it came from a more ecological self that was wider than my everyday self.

* * * * *** * * * *

If society as a whole is to be transformed, the spirituality of ecology cannot be confined to intellectuals like me writing books. The power of religion, and why it is so important for humanity at this present time, is its universality. This is why, in writing this book, I have laid such stress on the major faiths, rather than on the spirituality of new religious movements which, while important as the spearheads of change, are still a minority[108] in the population as a whole. Within the major faiths we can see openings for a unifying ecological vision and practice both in their existing traditions and in new practices that are emerging as a natural expression of existing beliefs.

In the Abrahamic religions (Judaism, Christianity and Islam) the concept of **creation** is vital to the religions and to ecology. This topic has become sadly distorted in recent times, as many strands within both science and religion have narrowed down their understanding of this concept to the point where "creation by God" and "evolution" have come to be seen as mutually exclusive. Part of the reason for this has been the growth of literalism in religion. Traditionally all the scriptures of "the people of the book" (as those of the Abrahamic faiths are called in the Qur'an) have been read on at least two levels, and usually on many levels. Judaism has developed an immense tradition of unfolding the inner meaning of scripture, culminating in the Kabbalah, which unfolds the symbolism of every word and letter of scripture. Christianity is based on the teaching of Jesus who, following in the tradition of rabbinical Judaism, used stories (parables) to convey his meaning by implication and allegory, so that the meaning was imprinted on the implicational as well as the propositional. In Islam a key text in the Qur'an (5:7) implies that parts are allegorical and parts literal, and the openness of the Arabic language used has allowed a succession of scholars to unfold further layers of meaning in addition to that which lies on the surface.

All these traditions have insisted that, in their common story that God "created the heavens and the earth in six days", a "day" did not mean 24 hours — which is obvious, since scripture also made clear that this measurement of time was not defined until there was a solar system with a regular alternation of day and night on the newly formed earth. Most importantly, the absolute distinction between creation by God and creation by natural causes could only emerge with the seventeenth century concept of a mechanical universe in which "natural causes" came to be seen as a completely closed and rigid mechanism, like clockwork, that left no place for any other principles for existence. Moreover (as we have seen in the previous chapters), God was not conceived as merely a master craftsman who shaped matter in the same way as did natural processes; but, in so far as it was possible to envisage God at all, God was the source of being itself. The influential 5th/6th century writer who wrote under the pseudonym "Dionysius the Areopagite" expressed this by saying that God was "above being" but that all creatures, including ourselves, derived their being by "participation" in God. This role of God as the source of being is summed up in the saying "God says 'be', and it is" which occurs repeatedly in the Qur'an[109], and I have explained in chapter 8 how this fits naturally into the picture emerging from modern science.

Recovering this traditional understanding of scripture makes it possible for the Abrahamic religions to embrace the physical world in its richness as a manifestation of sacred creativity, fully compatible with scientific ecology — an enterprise that has in the past been more immediately accessible for the Buddhist and Hindu traditions. A prominent exponent of this new understanding has been the American priest Matthew Fox, who has established the movement of "Creation centred spirituality" that now extends well beyond the confines of Christianity. I shall say more about this below. The American Baptist theologian John Dowd, in his book *Thank God for Evolution* has also done much to move beyond the distorted view of creationism.

A further example is the Islamic Foundation for Ecology and Environmental Sciences: an international organisation promoting responsible environmental action among Muslims. Their writings draw attention to the way the Qur'an emphasises the unity of human beings with the rest of the ecosystem, quoting such verses as "No creature is there crawling on the earth, no bird flying with its wings, but they are nations like unto yourselves. We have neglected nothing in the Book; then to their Lord they shall be mustered." (Qur'an 6:38). A major part of their work is teaching Muslims about their impact on the environment and the practical steps that can be taken to restore its health. Within the UK organisations such as Christian Ecology Link and Operation Noah are undertaking similar work.

*   *   * * *** *   *   *

We are talking here about turning around the whole planetary society, about 200 states and 6.7 billion people, hopefully within the next 20 years, if huge changes in climate are to be averted. Some might feel this feat to be like doing a wheelie with an oil tanker, but that would be to underestimate human ingenuity and resources. Globalisation (despite its many ills) has given humanity a potential for planetary transformation that would have been inconceivable only 20 years ago, and this gives us hope that we can make this transformation. Without hope nothing will be achieved, so let me very briefly sketch a few current trends on which we can build this hope.

- Both bottom-up change (small groups of people getting together to alter their own lives by local action) and top-down change is happening all the time. A very relevant example of bottom-up action is the transition towns movement in the UK. In 2005, building on 5 years of previous work in a local Further Education college, Rob Hopkins started an experimental programme in the town of Kinsale, in the Republic of Ireland[110]. Its aim was to lay down a process through which this one small town could, over a period of time, alter its economy so that it no longer pumped more carbon per person into the atmosphere than the planet could stand, and was no longer dependent on the huge quantities of oil that went into supplying both their energy needs and the plastics that went into making much of what they consumed. Those involved in the project became enthused and inspired by the positive changes of life that it suggested. They started to understand how these two linked goals, of reducing emissions and reducing oil use, were the key to living fruitfully on the earth; and in addition they discovered how they could make their local society more joyful and resilient, as they came together to work on small-scale actions that really made a difference. Life became more meaningful for them at all levels.

    This very small-scale project then inspired other groups of citizens to go further with the same ideas. Since the Kinsale project a cascade of actions for change has gathered momentum in towns, cities and larger areas throughout the UK and elsewhere. At the time of writing there are 186 such communities, towns and even cities[111] which are discovering with delight the path of "transition" – transition from a collection of individuals being driven by the destructive habits of the consumer society, to a community in the true sense of the word, finding both intellectual and spiritual fulfilment through being truly human in an ecological context.

• New hope is emerging for ending poverty and so enabling the poor who make up the majority of the population to participate in creating a better world.

Since, on the intuitive (implicational) side of our mind, our being is built from our relationships, we are impoverished whenever our relationships are fractured. And our society is today profoundly fractured into the rich and the poor. The rich have, in excess, power, mobility, food, shelter, health; the poor have none of these and feel excluded from the elites who control their lives. Though the way in which poverty is estimated is a contested area, some indication is given by figures such as, that in 2005 40% of the world's population live on less than $2 a day, and 20% of the population had 95% of the world income[112]. Moreover, this is not just a matter of rich versus poor nations, but also of inequality within nations. A compilation of recent research by Richard Wilkinson and Kate Pickett[113] now shows unambiguously that, once basic needs have been met, the most important driver of a range of social ills, from bad health to crime, is inequality. There can be little hope for a change towards a spiritual awareness of our living planet when the majority of the population have to struggle for their personal survival, or their self-esteem is undermined through gross and arbitrary social inequality. Society has the means, through our infrastructure, energy sources, international organisations and availability of labour, to end poverty. We even have a fair amount of will to end poverty, but we are addicted to economic systems (whether capitalist or theoretically "socialist") which systemically funnel the fruits of production to those who already have all they need.

Now, however, a variety of new economic systems, and some traditional ones, are coming into use and offering the possibility of real change:

- "Microfinance", first developed by Muhammad Yunis and others, is providing small-scale capital to enable men and, particularly, women in the poorest countries, who could never persuade conventional banks to give them a loan, to become independent traders and businesses.

- Islamic principles of economics are increasingly finding practical expression as a way of extending economic justice in the modern world. These forbid the charging of interest and stress the fundamental need to provide a livelihood for every member of the community.

- Christian and Jewish principles of justice, both stemming from an essential part of Biblical Law (see Deuteronomy), are finding expression through such organisations as the Christian Council for Monetary Justice[114].

- An overarching new economic theory embracing all these and several other innovations has taken shape in the form of the "Binary Economics" of Rodney Shakespeare and Louis Kelso[115]. This stabilises the money supply (which in reality has been essentially out of control) through the widespread use of interest-free loans for redistributing capital, and ensures that every individual has the means, through both income and capital, to have real access to the means of production. Until very recently conventional capitalism seemed far too well entrenched and apparently successful for it to allow the emergence of any alternative; but the recent global economic collapse has revealed its inadequacy and opened up a genuine interest in the alternatives.

There is no inevitable "evolution" sweeping us to a wonderful future. On the other hand it is not too late to change. We are not irredeemably corrupt, and change is not too difficult for us. We can change, and all these signs of hope give us evidence of this. The cosmos in its power and splendour provides all we need in order to move into our full humanity in harmony with the earth. It us up to us to accept this gift of the cosmos, and to take up our part in its constant ongoing weaving of itself.

Envoi

*I have come to the shore to inquire, What should I now say?
I touch the ocean wave, and the water to my forehead as if in blessing;
then ascend the headland seeking answer.*

*At each step I defer to the white snails in my path, their bodies white
and their shells white for traversing this chalky ground. Each step opens
to a wider view of the teeming busyness of the down: its many plants,
its swirling chattering birds, its scuttling rabbits. I have no need to
name them, but only to be speechless. Each one of them is sensitive at
every moment to exactly what in the surroundings concerns him now.*

*I am passing through a natural tree-arch, as to a sacred grove, then
sitting and knowing fleeting smells of fruit distilling from the damp
earth.*

*So, what should I say? Each one here brings me no message but
itself. And that is everything.*

Endnotes with references

1   The chorus of this song is in

▸ Starhawk, *The Spiral Dance*, HarperCollins, New York. 1979 and was subsequently developed orally. A version is in

▸ Kate Marks, *Circle of Song*, Windrush Publishing Services, Witney, UK, 1994, page 10

2   The main source for the myth of Eros and Psyche is from its inclusion in the bawdy novel The Golden Ass by the later Latin author Apuleius. See

▸ Lucius Apuleius Platonicus, *The Metamorphoses or Golden Ass of Apuleius of Madura*, trans. H. E. Butler (2 vols), Oxford University Press, Oxford, 1910

The significance of this myth for human integration and ecology has been deeply explored in

▸ Freya Mathews, *For Love of Matter: A contemporary panpsychism*, State University of New York Press, Albany NY, 2003

3   One drawback in eliminating the gods is that the story gets less racy. In the original, for instance, Aphrodite, at her first meeting with Psyche "leaped upon the face of poor Psyche, and, tearing her apparel, took her by the hair, and dashed her head upon the ground." (adapted from Apuleius, see note 2)

4   This concept of a dynamic flow between opposites was introduced in:

▸ June Boyce-Tillman, *Unconventional Wisdom (Gender, Theology and Spirituality)*, Equinox Publishing, London, 2008. See also a shortened version of her system in her chapter in

▸ Chris J S Clarke (ed.), *Ways of Knowing: Science and Mysticism Today*, Imprint Academic, Exeter, 2005. I am in this book applying her conception to slightly different categories, but many of her principles carry over into the treatment here.

5 ▶ Norma Kassi, "A Legacy of Maldevelopment: Environmental Devastation in the Arctic" in *Defending Mother Earth: Native American Perspectives on Environmental Justice*, Ed Jace Weaver, Orbis Books, Maryknoll NY, 1996, p. 75 (quoted in my edited book *Ways of knowing;* see note 4)

6 ▶ Jorge N Ferrer and Jacob H Sterman (ed.) *The participatory turn: spirituality, mysticism, religious studies* (ed.), SUNY Press, Albany NY, 2008 see especially pages 11 and 13.

7 ▶ Philip Barnard, "Asynchrony, implicational meaning and the experience of self in schizophrenia" in T Kircher & A. David (eds.), *The self in neuroscience and psychiatry*, pp. 121-146, Cambridge University Press, Cambridge, 2003

8 ▶ Marsha Linehan, *Skills Training Manual for Treating Borderline Personality Disorder*, The Guilford Press, New York, 1993 (see p. 66)

9 ▶ Tania Dolley, "Recovering our Animal Body", *GreenSpirit Journal*, **10** (1) pp. 9-11, 2008, online at http://www.greenspirit.org.uk/resources/animal_body.shtml

10 ▶ Carl Rogers, *On Becoming a Person: A Therapist's View of Psychotherapy*, Constable, London, 1967 see p105.

11 ▶ *The Bible*, Proverbs 8, 27-30, New International Version translation.

12 The union of opposites is a favourite theme of the psychologist C G Jung, a process that he calls enantiodromia. See p. 375 of:
▶ Carl G Jung, *Symbols of transformation: an analysis of the prelude to a case of schizophrenia*, trans. R F C Hull, Routledge and Kegan Paul, London, 1956.

13 ▶ Homer, *Illiad*, trans. Samuel Butler, Red and Black Publishers , St Petersburg, Fl USA, 2008 see **8**,13 ff. Tartarus

is mentioned in the ancient Christian hymn *Dies Irae* describing the fate of the dead, where there is the prayer "let them not be absorbed into Tartarus".

14 ▸ Jules Cashford & Nicholas Richardson (intro.), *Homeric Hymns*, Penguin Books, London, 2003. I am grateful to Jules Cashford for permission to publish this here. Note that there are two Homeric Hymns to Artemis: this is Hymn 27 in the Loeb edition of the Greek text. See p.452 of:

▸ Homer, *The Homeric Hymns and Homerica with an English Translation by Hugh G. Evelyn-White*, Heinemann, London, 1970 An on-line text is at

http://www.perseus.tufts.edu/hopper/text.jsp?doc=Perseus: text:1999.01.0137:hymn=27

15 This is a composite poem drawn from translations of Rumi by John Moyne, Coleman Barks and myself.

16 I am drawing this from Nagarjuna, following the approach of

▸ Robert Magliola, *Derrida on the mend*, Purdue University Press, West Lafayette Ind, USA, 1984

17 ▸ Isabel Clarke, *Madness, mystery and the survival of God*, O-Books, Winchester, UK, 2008

18 The separation of Church and State is usually traced back to the first amendment to the American Constitution, adopted in 1791, which states that "Congress shall make no law respecting an establishment of religion, or prohibiting the free exercise thereof; or abridging the freedom of speech, or of the press; or the right of the people peaceably to assemble, and to petition the Government for a redress of grievances." The concept of separation was crystallised by Jefferson in 1802 who described this amendment as a "wall of separation" between church and state. A strong influence on this had been the struggles between church and state in the French revolution during the 1790s (see http://en.wikipedia.org/wiki/Separation_of_church_and_st

ate)

19   Rumi, *Mathnawi* VI 2266, trans. Chittick. See p. 182 of:

▸ William C Chittick, *The Sufi Path of Love: The Spiritual Teachings of Rumi*, State University of New York Press, Albany NY, 1983

20   ▸ Reiner Schürmann, *Meister Eckhart, mystic and philosopher: translations with commentary*, Indiana University Press, Bloomington, 1978. See p. 219

21   ▸ Richard Dawkins, *The God Delusion*, Houghton Mifflin, Boston, 2008 (Chapter 1)

22   ▸ Ralph Waldo Emerson, *Nature and Selected Essays*, Penguin Classics, New York, 2003 See "Nature," Chapter 5

23   ▸ John Muir, *John of the Mountains*, ed. Linnie Marsh Wolfe, Houghton Mifflin Company, Boston, 1938. See p. 39

24   I use the word 'Hinduism' here for brevity, but it should be remembered that the word is a European invention from the nineteenth century, referring vaguely to the religion of those who lived in 'Hindustan', a term for Northern India. It refers to a family of practices and ideas rather than to a single defined religion.

25   Extracts from *Rig Veda* 10:37 as translated in:

▸ Raimon Pannikar, *The Vedic Experience Mantramañjari: An Anthology Of The Vedas For Modern Man*, University of California Press, Berkeley, 1977

26   *Rig Veda* 2:62, usually held to be part of the oldest core of the text. See Pannikar, note 25

27   ▸ Karen Armstrong, *The Great Transformation: The Beginning of Our Religious Traditions*, Atlantic, London, 2006. See p. 69

28   ▸ James Bennett Pritchard (ed.), *The Ancient Near East - Volume 1: An Anthology of Texts and Pictures.* Princeton University Press, Princeton, 1958.

29   ▸ *The Bible*, Psalm 104, 20-24

30   ▸ *The Bible*, Deuteronomy 6, 4

31 The chronology of Indian religious texts is notoriously problematic, since (unlike the Hebrew texts) they carry few historical references that can be validated archaeologically. The dates given here are mainly from Armstrong, see note 27.

32 The gîva, or living Self in the mind: see VI.3: 2 of this Upanishad.

33 Chandogya Upanishad VI.8 verses 2, 6, 7 from:
> ▸ *The Sacred Books of the East: Volume 1. The Upanishads. Part 1*, Trans. Friedrich Max Muller, Adamant Media Corporation, Boston, 2000 [1879]

34 Brihadaranyaka Upanishad, 4.4.5 11.5:19 from:
> ▸ Robert Hume, *The Thirteen Principal Upanishads*, Oxford University Press, Oxford, 1931.

35 ▸ Thich Nhat Hahn, *The path of emancipation: Talks from a 21-day mindfulness retreat*, Parallax Press, Berkeley, 2000

36 ▸ Francis H Cook, *Hua-Yen Buddhism: The Jewel Net of Indra*, Pennsylvania State University Press, University Park,1977. See p. 2. This retelling by Cook sums up the implications of a number of traditional texts. The main source is usually cited as the Avatamsaka Sutra, which has survived only in Chinese translations. An English translation of the Chinese version by Shikshananda (652-710 CE), lacking the detail in Cook's version, is in:
> ▸ Thomas Cleary, *The Flower Ornament Scripture: A Translation of the Avatamsaka Sutra*, Shambhala , Boston, 1987 (See Vol 1, p. 368 for this legend)

37 See Joanna Macy's website article http://www.joannamacy.net/html/buddhism/interdependence.html

38 *The Bible*, 1 John 8, 4

39 *The Bible*, 1 Corinthians 13, 4-8

40 *The Bible*, Psalm 86, 15

41 *The Qur'an*, 3, 31 (Asad translation)

42 *Dīwān-i Shams-i Tabrīzī*, 8226-28 trans. Chittick (adapted): see note 19, p. 299.

43 ‣ Annemarie Schimmel, *Mystische Dimensionen des Islam: Die Geschichte des Sufismus*, E. Diederichs, Cologne, 1985, pp240-41, translated in:

‣ Dorothee Soelle, *The Silent Cry: Mysticism and Resistance*, trans Barbara and Martin Rumscheidt, Fortress Press, Minneapolis, 2001, p 35

44 ‣ Margaret Smith, *The Way of the Mystics: The Early Christian Mystics and the Rise of the Sufis*, Oxford University Press, Oxford, 1978, p. 224.

45 *The Bible,* 1 Corinthians 11 is one of the most influential of his reports.

46 The meanings of the terms used here are subtle: there are three levels of "same" involved here: same in essence (*ousia*) according to which the Son the Father and the Spirit are "the same"; same in *hypostasis* according to which the Father, Son and Spirit are different; and same in nature (*physis*) according to which the Son has two different natures, God and Human. A particularly confusing factor, however, is that the literal Latin equivalent of *hypostasis* was *substantia*, from which we get the English "substance". Historically, however, *substantia* was used as the Latin translation of *ousia*, not of *hypostasis*, so that in the English creed Christians say that the Son has the same "substance" as the Father. To make things even more confusing, in later writings the rather unsatisfactory word "person" was used as an equivalent to *hypostasis*. For more details see:

‣ G Christopher Stead, *Divine substance* , Clarendon Press, Oxford, 1977

47 Duino Elegies 1: "Denn das Schöne ist nichts / als des Schrecklichen Anfang, den wir noch grade ertragen". For text and an alternative translation see p.2 of:

‣ Rainer Maria Rilke *Duino Elegies*, with trans. C F

MacIntyre, University of California Press, Berkeley, 1961

48 For the relation between Socrates and Plato see *Was Socrates a Mystic?* by Mike King:
http://www.jnani.org/mrking/writings/essays/essaysukc/download/SOCMYS1.RTF

49 See

▸ James Hankins, "Plato in the Middlee Ages" in J Strayer (ed.), *Dictionary of the Middle Ages*, vol IX, Scribner, New York 1987 (pp 694-704)
http://www.scribd.com/doc/7878958/Hankins-Plato-in-the-Middle-Ages

50 There is an interesting partial parallel between Plato's forms and Rupert Sheldrake's formative causation. Sheldrake is Platonic in that he assumes there is such a thing as the "form" of any object or action (without ever making it very clear what it is), and that the form can play a part in bringing that thing into existence. But, unlike Plato, Sheldrake insists that forms are always derived by development from previous forms, transmitted to a later time by the "morphogenetic field". Plato's forms are eternal while Sheldrake's are evolutionary. See:

▸ Rupert Sheldrake, *A new science of life: the hypothesis of formative causation*, Blond & Briggs, London 1981

51 These quotation are from the translation of the Timaeus in:

▸ Plato, *The Dialogues of Plato translated into English, with analyses and introductions*, B. Jowett. 3rd ed., Clarendon, Oxford, 1892.

52 The unanswered problem of how soul and body were related was well expressed in a letter from Princess Elizabeth to Descartes (written May 6-16, 1643): "I beg of you to tell me how the human soul can determine the movement of the animal spirits in the body so as to perform voluntary acts — being as it is merely a conscious substance. For the determination of movement seems

always to come about from the moving body's being propelled — to depend on the kind of impulse it gets from what sets it in motion, or again, on the nature and shape of this latter thing's surface. Now the first two conditions involve contact, and the third involves that the impelling thing has extension; but you utterly exclude extension from your notion of soul, and contact seems to me incompatible with a thing's being immaterial." Descartes attempts to reply, but the worry seems to many to remain. See

▸ René Descartes *Philosophical Writings*, ed. Anscombe and Geach, ed., Nelson, Edinburgh, 1964, pp. 274-75.

http://www.trinity.edu/cbrown/modern/descartesMajor Points.html

53 Descartes' tactical reticence in venturing into theology is expressed by such paragraphs as: "Thus, if perhaps God reveal to us or others, matters concerning himself which surpass the natural powers of our mind, such as the mysteries of the incarnation and of the trinity, we will not refuse to believe them, although we may not clearly understand them." *The principles of philosophy* XXV:

▸ René Descartes, *Descartes: A Discourse on Method Meditations and Principles*, translated by John Veitch, Dent, London, 1960

54 "Dû solt alzemâle entsinken dîne dînesheit unde solt zerfliesen in sîne sînesheit unde sol dîn dîn in sînem mîn ein mîn werden alse genzlich, daz dû mit ime verstandest êwiclîche sîne ungewordene istikeit unde sîne ungenanten nihtheit." From

▸ Franz Pfeiffer, *Deutsche Mystiker des vierzehnten Jahrhunderts* , Scientia, Aalen, 1962; Vol 2, Sermon XCIX, p.319 l.18 ff, Translation adapted from

▸ Matthew Fox, *Breakthrough: Meister Eckhart's Creation Spirituality in New Translation*, Doubleday, New York, 1980, p179

55 Fox, note 54, p.217. Eckhart has "Her umbe sô bite ich got, daz er mich ledic mache gotes, wan mîn wesenlich wesen ist ober got ...": "Therefore I pray God to make me free of God, because my essential being is above God ..." (Pfeiffer [note 54] Sermon LXXXVII, p. 283, l.37, with correction from

▸ *Meister Eckart: die Deutscher Werke* ed. Josef Quint, Stuttgart, 1958-76, vol II, p 52 ll. 16-17

56 I use "overflowing" to represent Eckhart's term "ebullitio" (boiling over), referring first to the emanation of the Son from the Father, and the reabsorbtion of the Son, and secondly referring to the act of creation.

▸ Meister Eckhart, *Werke II, Bibliothek des Mittelalters bd. 21,* Deutscher Klassiker Verlag, Frankfurt am Main, 1993, p 602 ll. 14-18

57 "Mê sprich ich: got muoz vil bî ich werden und ich vil bî got, alse gar ein, daz diz er unde diz ich ein ist, werden unde sint, und in der istikeit êwiclîche ein werc wirkent". Pfeiffer [note 54] Sermon XCIX, p. 320 l. 11; Quint [note 55] 83, p 194, ll. 10-14. Translation from Fox [note 54] , p. 180

58 Plato's term for the ultimate source of value is *to agathon,* "The Good", which takes cosmological form in the *Cosmographia* of Bernardus Silvertris, a mediaeval version of the Artemis myth. Matter is there called "Silva", the Latin for wood and hence a translation of the Greek *hule* in the sense of matter, and the supreme form is called "Tougathon" from *to agathon.* Bernardus' allegory has been a strong inspiration for this book. See:

▸ Bernard Silvestris, *The Cosmographia of Bernardus Silvestris / A translation with introd. and notes by Winthrop Wetherbee,* Columbia University Press, New York, 1973.

59 "Que bien sé yo la fonte que mana y corre, / Aunque es de noche. / ... Su claridad nunca es escurecida, / Y sé que toda luz de ella es venida, / Aunque es de noche."

▸ St John of the Cross, *The Poems of St John of the Cross; The*

Spanish text with a translation by Roy Campbell, Harvill Press, London, 1951 # VIII pp. 44-47: "Cantar del anima que se huelga de conoscer a Dios por fe."

60 ▸ Joel R Primack and Nancy Ellen Abrams, *The View from the Center of the Universe: Discovering Our Extraordinary Place in the Cosmos,* Riverhead Hardcover, New York, 2006 http://viewfromthecenter.com/figures/index.html

61 "'What is truth?' asked jesting Pilate, but would not stay for answer". Francis Bacon, *Essays,* "On Truth"

62 For an overview of the philosophy of truth, see http://plato.stanford.edu/entries/truth/

63 ▸ Karen Armstrong, *The Great Transformation, the world in the time of Buddha, Socrates, Confucius and Jeremiah,* Atlantic Books, 2006

64 Karen Armstrong (Note 63) pp. 145-6, quoting Mary Douglas, *Leviticus as Literature*

65 "Modum ergo tradere aggredior, quo semper homines ratio-cinationes suas in omni argumento ad calculi formam exhibere controversiasque omnes finire possunt, ut non jam clamoribus rem agere necesse sit, sed alter alteri dicere possit: calculemus." From *Guilielmi Pacidii initia et specimina Scientiae generalis:*

▸ Gottfried Wilhelm Leibniz, *Sämtliche Schriften und Briefe, Herausgegeben von der Berlin-Brandenbergischen Akademie der Wissenschaften und der Akademie der Wissenschaften in Göttingen,* VIe Reihe, 4e Band, Teil A (1999), pp 492-3, ll. 22-24

66 "Now I say that whenever I conceive any material or corporeal substance, I immediately feel the need to think of it as bounded, and as having this or that shape; as being large or small in relation to other things, and in some specific place at any given time; as being in motion or at rest; as touching or not touching some other body; and as being one in number, or few, or many. From these conditions I

cannot separate such a substance by any stretch of my imagination. But that it must be white or red, bitter or sweet, noisy or silent, and of sweet or foul odour, my mind does not feel compelled to bring in as necessary accompaniments. Without the senses as our guides, reason or imagination unaided would probably never arrive at qualities like these. Hence I think that tastes, odors, colors, and so on are no more than mere names so far as the object in which we place them is concerned, and that they reside only in the consciousness. Hence, if the living creature were removed, all these qualities would be wiped away and annihilated." Galileo, *The Assayer* in:

▶ Galileo, *Discoveries and Opinions of Galileo*, trans. Stillman Drake, Doubleday, New York, 1957 [1623], p.274-7

67 ▶ Ignacio Matte Blanco, *The Unconscious as Infinite Sets*, Karnac Books, London, 1975

68 For an account in greater depth of the personalities and physics involved in this conference, see:

▶ Manjit Kumar, *Quantum: Einstein, Bohr and the great debate about the nature of reality*, Icon Books, Thriplow, UK, 2008

69 Demonstrated by Johann Balmer in 1885

70 Cleve has argued that Pythogoras' conception of number (ca 575 – 490 BCE) made numbers discrete constituents of the universe. See

▶ Felix M Cleve, *The Giants Of Pre-Sophistic Greek Philosophy: An Attempt to Reconstruct Their Thoughts*, Martinus Nijhoff Publishers, The Hague, 1965.

Subsequently Empedocles (ca 490 – 430 BCE) continued the idea of a universe with a number of distinct constituents while Democritos (ca 460-370 BCE) formulated what became the definition of "atomism" - a universe generated by the random motion of particles in a void - and Plato (ca 428 – 348 BCE) moved towards a concept of basic elements that had distinct shapes. The idea of atoms was highly influential in post-renaissance Europe through the poetry of Lucretius (ca 99 – 55 BCE). See

▸ Robert H Kargon, *Atomism in England from Hariot to Newton*, Oxford U.P, Oxford, 1966

The idea of a continuous universe seems to have been present in the works of Thales (ca 624 – 546 BCE), who held that water was the basic constituent, and Anaximander (ca 610 – 546 BCE).

71 ▸ Niels Bohr, "Discussion with Einstein on epistemological problems in atomic physics" in *Albert Einstein: Philosopher-Scientist"* ed. Paul Arthur Schilpp, Library of Living Philosophers, Evanston, Ill, 1949, pp 201-241. This quotation is from page 218.

72 ▸ Garrett Birkhoff and John von Neumann, "The Logic of Quantum Mechanics", *Annals of Mathematics*, vol **37** pp. 823 – 843, 1936.

73 The phrase was coined by Arthur Young, the inventor of the Bell helicopter, in a private conversation.

74 ▸ Christopher J Isham and C Jeremy Butterfield, "Topos perspective on the Kochen-Specker theorem: I. Quantum states as generalized valuations," *Int J Theor Phys*, 1998, vol **37**, pages 2669 – 2733

75 ▸ Robert Goldblatt, *Topoi: the categorial analysis of logic,* North-Holland, Amsterdam , 1984

76 See note 94 below.

77 ▸ Laurie Lee, *The Bloom of Candles: Verse from a Poet's Year,* London: John Lehmann, 1947.

Another example of the power of the implicational to unite the part and the whole, and hence unite opposites, is the Italian section of the lyrics of the song "Allegria" by Gypsy Kings on the CD:

▸ Gyspy Kings, *Allegria*, Nonesuch , ASIN: B000002H8R, Track 5

Translation: "Joy / Like a flash of life / Joy / Like the cry of a fool / Joy / An outrageous cry / Beautiful, roaring pain / Serene / Like the raging of love / Joy / Like an assault of delight"

78 'For him, what was needed was an account in which "physical facts will be physically explained", where by "physically explained" he meant that the explanation should involve general physical principles, not necessarily mechanical devices. He felt he had reached this when he defined the "electromagnetic field" as "the space in the neighbourhood of the electric and magnetic bodies" which had the capacity for "becoming the receptacle for two forms of energy", namely energy of motion (kinetic energy) and stored "potential" energy.' See:

▸ Stathis Psillos, *Scientific Realism: How Science Tracks Truth,* Routledge, London, 1999, pp. 132-133; his refs: (1861 p 486), (1855, 155), (1873:432))

79 In classical systems also one can introduce a more general notion of a state that gives probabilities, rather than always giving exact values, so that the previous notion of a classical state then becomes the special case of a classical "probability-state", as I shall call it, in which all the probabilities are either 1 (certainty) or zero (impossibility). This probability state is represented by a rule (strictly speaking, a generalised function) that assigns a probability to any (ordinary classical) states. This gives rise to a very confusing situation! If one does quantisation by using the ★ product described in the following note, then one also represents (quantum) states by a generalised function of classical states; but the generalised functions are different: in the quantum case they can be negative, for instance, and the probabilities for actual measurements are computed differently in the classical and quantum cases.

80 The word "algebra" has, unfortunately, a multitude of meanings: here it means a collection of mathematical

entities (represented below by the letters A, B, C etc) which admit the following operations

They can be added, to produce $A + B$ etc

There is a special entity 0 such that $0 + A = A$

For each A there is an entity $-A$ such that $A + -A = 0$. (The left hand side of this is written as $A - A$, for convenience)

They can be multiplied by any complex (or real) number a to produce aA etc.

They can be multiplied by each other producing $A \times B$ (more usually written AB).

These operations obey a long list of rules, essentially all you might expect including $A + B = B + A$ *but not* $A \times B = B \times A$ (though this might happen as a special sort of algebra, or for particular entities in the algebra).

The traditional entities to choose for this is a set of mathematical transformations (usually called "operators") that move the quantum states (or wave-functions) around. These are not physical movements to be found in the world, but merely hypothetical operations used to construct the requisite algebra. In 1946 a more natural representation was found by Groenewold (and independently later discovered by Moyal, after whom it is named), using just a modification of the usual algebra obeyed by the properties in a classical system. Here the classical system is represented as a mathematical "space" of all possible states of the system, which is usually all possible positions and momenta, and a *quantity A* (i.e. a physical property) is a rule (called, more formally, a "function") that for each state s produces a number written as $A(s)$. Any two such functions can by multiplied by other numbers and can be multiplied by each other: AB is just the function that produces the number $A(s) B(s)$ when applied to the state s. This algebra *does* satisfy $AB = BA$. Suppose, however, one now modifies this multiplication to a new form (here denoted by $\star$) which, in the special case where there is just one position dimension x and one momentum coordinate p, takes the form of an infinite series whose first terms are given by

$$A \star B = AB + (i\hbar/2)(A_x B_p - A_p B_x) - \ldots$$

Here "A_x" means the rate of change of A in the direction of the position dimension and "A_p" means the rate of change in the direction of the momentum dimension. Subsequent terms involve rates-of-change-of-rates-of-change, and so on. (The constant $\hbar$, called "the reduced Planck constant" is a fundamental constant of the universe that specifies the size of the "crack" in everything.) Then this algebra is the algebra of quantum theory, in which *complementary* properties (in Bohr's sense) obey the algebra-equivalent of Heisenberg's uncertainty relation: $A \star B - B \star A = i\hbar$. While this version of quantisation is conceptually appealing, as being simply a "deformation" of the classical situation, the conventional version is computationally a lot easier.

81 ▸ Werner Heisenberg, *Der Teil und das Ganze*, Piper, Munich, 1969, translated and quoted in http://en.wikipedia.org/wiki/Matrix_mechanics

82 For an exposition and alternative view of the interplay between the quantum formalism and actual creative manifestation see:

▸ Roland Omnès, *Quantum Philosophy: Understanding and Interpreting Contemporary Science,* English Edition, Princeton University Press, Princeton NJ, 1999.

He argues that quantum theory depended on two aspects: "Logos" (the formalism of quantum field) and "reality" - the particular aspect of the world that emerges in each moment. (The terminology is unfortunate in our context here because "Logos" is also used in Christian scripture to denote the essence of creativity, which is opposite to "Logos" in Omnès' sense.) For Omnès this act of emergence has no explanation, and needs no explanation. It is beyond what he calls "Logos" and so cannot be probed. Indeed, he condemns all attempts to go beyond this veil as "nonsense, twaddle, balderdash, and idle fancies" (p. 198). Thus, like many physicists, he appears (at least in print) to have a complete separation between the rational (his "Logos") and the intuitive, and so he can neither explore the intuitive, nor admit that it could be the source of his "Reality".

83 ▸ Stuart Kaufmann, *Reinventing the Sacred: A New View of Science, Reason, and Religion*, Basic Books, New York, 2008

84 See Lyn Andrews: www.philosophicfriend.org

85 I follow here the approach to Kant of
▸ Anthony Savile, *Kant's Critique of Pure Reason: an orientation to the central theme*, Blackwell, Malden MA, 2005

86 I translate Kant's *Anschauungen*, normally translated as "intuitions", as "manifestations" in order to avoid confusion with "intuition" as an alternative name for the capacity of the implicational subsystem described in Chapter 9

87 ▸ John D Teasdale and Philip J Barnard, *Affect, Cognition and Change*, Laurence Erlbaum Associates, London, 1995

88 ▸ Philip J Barnard "Bridging between basic theory and clinical practice", *Behaviour Research and Therapy*, **42**, 977-1000, 2004

89 ▸ The visual cortex of the brain, for example, is a complete processing system in its own right. Although analogous to an ICS subsystem, it is at a lower level in not having a searchable memory or translation mechanisms to communicate with the other subsystems in their own "codes".

90 See Teasdale and Barnard (Note 87) Chapter 9.

91 There are two sorts of memory in ICS: the "image" which is just a snapshot of the present situation, and a more structured "record" resulting from a subsystem working on successive images, comparing them with existing records, and modifying the whole set as a result. It is these more structured records, which for IMPLIC are sometimes called

"schemata" that build up the sense of self.

92   Isabel Clarke, "Cognitive Therapy and Serious Mental Illness. An interacting Cognitive Subsystems Approach", *Clinical Psychology and Psychotherapy*, **6**, 375 – 383, 1999, see page 378.

93   ▸ Matthew Fox, *Original Blessing* Bear & Company, Santa Fe, 1983.

I am here drawing on the detailed development of this idea in:

▸ Isabel Clarke, "The Ecopsychology of Matthew Fox's Four Ways", *GreenSpirit*, **10** (1) pp. 12-15, 2008

94   ▸ Farhad Dalal, *Taking the Group Seriously*, Jessica Kingsley, London, 1998, pp. 180-181

95   *Nature* (editorial material), **378**, 524 (7 December), 1995

96   *Nature* (editorial material), **378**, 759 (21/28 December), 1995

97   Misunderstanding of the meaning of climate change is still tragically widespread. I frequently hear it said from people of all political hues that there remains significant uncertainty as to "whether global warming is caused by human activity". This is a nonsensical question, like the question of whether lung cancer is caused by smoking: in both cases, human action is not a single cause, but it greatly exacerbates something that is also affected by non-human factors. What is now clear is that *if human activity does not change, the earth's temperature averaged over a year and over the globe will, in the second half of this century, be at least 4°C higher than it otherwise would be,* and that the consequences of this for agriculture and human activity as we know it would be catastrophic. The only uncertainty lies in exactly which areas will be affected and when. For the evidence, now overwhelming, of these facts see Chapter 10 of the *IPCC Fourth Assessment Report: Working Group I Report "The Physical Science Basis"* at http://www.ipcc.ch/pdf/assessment-report/ar4/wg1/ar4-

wg1-chapter10.pdf

98 See *Oxford English Dictionary*, "Ecology" and "eco-"

99 ▸ B Alan Wallace, *Hidden dimensions: the unification of physics and consciousness*, Columbia University Press, New York, 2007

100 ▸ Stuart Hameroff & Roger Penrose, "Orchestrated Reduction Of Quantum Coherence In Brain Microtubules: A Model For Consciousness?" in: *Toward a Science of Consciousness - The First Tucson Discussions and Debates*, eds. Hameroff, S R, Kaszniak, AW and Scott, AC, MIT Press, Cambridge, MA, pp. 507-540, 1996

101 ▸ Henry O Stapp. "Quantum interactive dualism: An alternative to materialism", *J. Consc. Studies*, **12**, 43-58, 2005

102 ▸ Chris J S Clarke "The role of quantum physics in the theory of subjective consciousness", *Mind and Matter*, **5**, 45-82, 2007

103 The Bible, Proverbs 8,22-23, 30-31, New International Version

A much richer mythic picture of this is to be found in the Jewish Kabalistic tradition, as described in:

▸ Brian L Lancaster "Engaging with the Mind of God: The Participatory Path of Jewish Mysticism" in Ferrer, *The participatory turn* (note 6).

This shows that it is much too simplistic to equate God with form and Hokmah with being, indeed, these categories do not really carry over into the more fundamental realm that is accessed in mystical awareness.

104 One of the most useful formulations of the interaction of being and meaning is in Chapter 3 of:

▸ David Bohm, *Unfolding Meaning: a weekend of dialogue*, ed. Donald Factor, Foundation House, Mickleton, 1985

105 ▸ Arne Naess, "Identification as a source of deep ecological attitudes" in M. Tobias, ed., *Deep Ecology*. Avant Books, San Diego, pp.256-270, 1985.

106 ▸ Elizabeth Ann Bragg, "Towards Ecological Self: deep ecology meets constructionist self-theory", *Journal of Environmental Psycholog,y* **16**, 93–108, 1996

107 For a passionate exposition of this perversion of Islam, see:
▸ Ayaan Hirsi Ali *Infidel,* Simon and Schuster, London, 2007

108 The influence of new religious movements is further weakened by their fragmentation. In the UK a hopeful move towards ending this is being developed by the Foundation for Holistic Spirituality — www.holisticmap.org and www.f4hs.org – which is working to bring these groups together. A common basis for such groups is being developed by the Wrekin Forum, www.wrekinforum.org

109 E.g. "when He wills a thing to be, He but says unto it 'Be' – and it is" (Qur'an, 2,117, Assad translation)

110 ▸ Rob Hopkins, *The Transition Handbook: from oil dependency to local resilience*, Green Books, Totnes, 2008, p. 122

111 See http://transitiontowns.org/TransitionNetwork/Transition Communities

112 See http://www.globalissues.org/article/26/poverty-facts-and-stats

113 ▸ Richard Wilkinson and Kate Pickett *The Spirit Level: Why More Equal Societies Almost Always Do Better,* Allen Lane, London, 2009

114 See http://www.ccmj.org/

115 ▸ Rodney Shakespear and Peter Challen, *Seven Steps to Justice,* New European Publications, London, 2002

BOOKS